$109\frac{5}{x}$

The Archeology of the Frivolous

Duquesne Studies —Philosophical Series

Volume Thirty-Seven

André Schuwer and John Sallis, *editors*

JACQUES DERRIDA

The Archeology of the Frivolous

Reading Condillac

Translated
With an Introduction
by
JOHN P. LEAVEY, JR.

DUQUESNE UNIVERSITY PRESS

PITTSBURGH

First published in 1973 as
L'archéologie du frivole
Copyright 1973 by Editions Galilée, Paris

Translation Copyright © 1980 by Duquesne University Press

Published by Duquesne University Press
600 Forbes Avenue, Pittsburgh, PA 15219
Distributed by Humanities Press
Atlantic Highlands, New Jersey 07716

First Edition

Library of Congress Cataloging in Publication Data

Derrida, Jacques.
    The archeology of the frivolous.

    (Duquesne studies : Philosophical series ; v. 37)
    Translation of L'archéologie du frivole, which was first published in 1973 with
E.B. de Condillac's Essai sur l'origine des connaissances humaines and reprinted
separately in 1976.
    Includes bibliographical references and index.
    1. Condillac, Étienne Bonnot de, 1714-1780. Essai sur l'origine des connais-
sances humaines. 2. Psychology—Early works to 1850. 3 Knowledge, Theory
of. 4. Languages—Philosophy. I. Title. II. Series.
B1983.E83D4713   121   80-23620
ISBN 0-391-01636-9

CONTENTS

) 1
the fractured frame, the seduction of fiction (

) 2
parenthesis (

"(I read while writing: slowly, taking pleasure in prefacing at length each term)" ("Positions," in *Diacritics*, 3, 1973, p. 43).

) 3
the preface (

The preface—and also the act of prefacing—has been a key to understanding Derrida's complex writing. In her preface to the translation of Derrida's *Of Grammatology*, Gayatri Spivak begins: "If you have been reading Derrida, you will know that a plausible gesture would be to begin with a consideration of 'the question of the preface.'" Her sometimes exotic text continues with citations of both Hegel's indictment of reading (and writing) prefaces in philosophical works and the supporting speculations of his French translator and commentator, Jean Hyppolite. Then she writes:

> A written preface provisionally localizes the place where, between reading and reading, book and book, the inter-inscribing of "reader(s)," "writer(s)," and language is forever at work. Hegel had closed the circle between father and son, text and preface. He had in fact suggested, as Derrida makes clear, that the fulfilled concept—the end of

the self-acting method of the philosophical text—was the pre-dicate—pre-saying—pre-face, to the preface. In Derrida's reworking, the structure preface-text becomes open at both ends. The text has no stable identity, no stable origin, no stable end. Each act of reading the "text" is a preface to the next. The reading of a self-professed preface is no exception to this rule. (*Grammatology*, p. xii)

Later, ending her epigraphical remarks, she concludes: "There is, then, always already a preface between two hands holding open a book. And the 'prefacer,' of the same or another proper name as the 'author,' need not apologize for 'repeating' the text" (ibid., p. xiii).

) 4
the introduction (

Most likely written in 1974 (with additions and emendations throughout 1975), Spivak's preface states what continues to be true of *L'Archéologie du frivole,* first published in 1973 and herein translated. In her list of the texts published by Derrida, Spivak observes: "There was a little noticed introduction to the *Essai sur l'origine des connaissances humaines* by Condillac" (ibid., p. ix).

But why call this text an introduction? Especially given Derrida's parenthetical remark above and Spivak's preface. Are the introduction and the preface the same? different? coincidental?

In the original version of the *Archéologie* published with Condillac's *Essai,* Derrida's text simply precedes Condillac's:

3

"précédé de *L'archéologie du frivole* par Jacques Derrida." Not until the section constituting a "marginal note or remark," the section on "two loose pages," does Derrida partly reveal his hand: "You have already remarked that this *alleged Introduction* . . ." (p. 108 below; my emphasis).

* * *

(Note: *Fors* "precedes" Abraham and Torok's *Cryptonymie* (1976), but seems to do so, according to Derrida, as a prefatory precedence (one that does not even enter into the Table des Matières): "What is a crypt?

"All that can be said against a preface, I have already said. The place of what absence—of what of whom of what lost text—does the preface claim to take? Thus disposing and predisposing (of) a first word that does not belong to it, the preface—a crypt in its turn—will take the form of what pre-serves (and ob-serves me here), the irreplaceable.

"I shall not engage myself beyond this first word in (the) place of an other" (trans. Barbara Johnson, in *Georgia Review,* 31, 1977, p. 65).

I do not know about *Scribble*.

But *Edmund Husserl's "Origin of Geometry": An Introduction* is simply labeled introduction: "In the introduction we now attempt, our sole ambition will be to recognize and situate one stage of Husserl's thought, with its specific presuppositions and its particular unfinished state" (p. 27). Published in France in 1962, this is Derrida's "first extended work," not *Speech and Phenomena* as Said inaccurately states (and thereby misconstrues) in "The Problem of Textuality: Two Exemplary Positions," *Critical Inquiry,* 4, 1978, p. 684.

Published five years after the introduction to *The Origin of Geometry, Speech and Phenomena* is subtitled *Introduction to the Problem of Signs in Husserl's Phenomenology.*

I do not know whether "+ R (par dessus le marché)" is simply added to Adami's work, includes it, introduces, or even prefaces it.

4

Grammatology contains the "Introduction to the 'Age of Rousseau' ": "This work will present itself gradually. I cannot therefore justify it by way of anticipation and preface. Let us nevertheless attempt an overture" (p. 97).

Two of Derrida's texts on Hegel are introductions, but "Hors livre" is undecided on this: "Le Puits et la pyramide: Introduction à la sémiologie de Hegel" and *Glas: "Einführung* . . . introduction *into* Hegel" (p. 10).

Derrida's latest introduction, "Me—Psychoanalysis: An Introduction to the Translation of 'The Shell and the Kernel' by Nicolas Abraham," develops the turn of *Glas*: "I am introducing here—me—(into) a translation.

"That says clearly enough to what lengths I will be taken by these double voice-tracks [*voies*]: to the point of effacing myself on the threshold in order to facilitate your reading. I'm writing in 'my' language but in your idiom I have to *introduce*. Or otherwise, and again in 'my' language, to *present* someone. Someone who in numerous and altogether singular ways is not there and yet is close and present enough not to require an introduction" (trans. Nicholas Rand, in *Diacritics*, 9, 1979, p. 4).)

* * *

) 5
circumstances (

In 1972 Derrida discusses the difference between the Hegelian preface (*Vorrede*) and introduction (*Einleitung*). In "Hors livre: Préfaces," the only previously unpublished text included in *La Dissémination,* he writes:

> We must distinguish the *preface* from the *introduction*. They do not have the same function or dignity in Hegel's eyes, although they pose an analogous problem in their relation to the philosophical corpus of the exposition. The Introduction (*Einleitung*) has a more systematic, less historical, less circumstantial bond to the logic of the book. The Introduction is *unique*, deals with the general and essential architectonic problems, and presents the general concept in its division and self-differentiation. Prefaces, on the contrary, multiply from edition to edition and take into account a more empiric historicity. They respond to a necessity of circumstance Hegel defines, of course, *in a preface....*
> (*Dissémination*, p. 23)

According to *circumstance,* Hegel's now famous Preface to the *Phenomenology of Spirit* joins the *Phenomenology* to the *Science of Logic*. The Preface was written after the *Phenomenology* but before the *Logic*. In *Genesis and Structure of Hegel's "Phenomenology of Spirit,"* Hyppolite elucidates: "We know that Hegel wrote the preface to the *Phenomenology* after he had finished the book, when he was able to take stock of his 'voyage of discovery.' It was meant primarily to establish the connection between the *Phenomenology,* which, by itself, appears as the 'first part of science,' and the *Wissenschaft der Logik* . . . which, from a different perspective, is to constitute the first moment of an encyclopedia" (trans. Samuel Cherniak and John Heckman, Northwestern, 1974, p. 3).

According to another *circumstance*: "The introduction to the *Phenomenology*, however, was conceived at the same time as the book itself, and written first. It seems to contain the original thought from which the whole work emerged" (ibid., pp. 3–4).

) 6
logics (

Hegel interjects a philosophical objection to these circumstances (Derrida also cites this passage in "Hors livre"): "For whatever might appropriately be said about philosophy in a preface—say a historical *statement* of the main drift and the point of view, the general content and results, a string of random assertions and assurances about truth—none of this can be accepted as the way in which to expound philosophical truth." The previous two sentences of the *Phenomenology* clarify this objection: "It is customary to preface a work with an explanation of the author's aim, why he wrote the book, and the relationship in which he believes it to stand to other earlier or contemporary treatises on the same subject. In the case of a philosophical work, however, such an explanation seems not only *superfluous* but, in view of the nature of the subject-matter, even inappropriate and misleading" (trans. A. V. Miller, Oxford, 1977, p. 1; my emphasis).

And it is known Hegel asserted "there can be no introduction to philosophy" (Hyppolite's *Genesis and Structure*, pp. 53 and 55).

Hyppolite summarizes the logical distinction between the introduction and the preface as follows: "The preface is an hors d'oeuvre; it contains general information on the goal that Hegel set for himself and on the relation between his work and other philosophic treatises on the same subject. The introduction, on the contrary, is an integral part of the book: it poses and locates the problem, and it determines the means to resolve it" (ibid., p. 4).

THE FRACTURED FRAME

* * *

(The preface as hors d'oeuvre requires integration with Derrida's work on the *parergon* in *La Vérité en peinture*: "A *parergon* without *ergon*? A 'pure' supplement? Clothing as 'bare' supplement of the 'nude' . . . ? A supplement with nothing to supplement, naming, on the contrary, what it supplies . . . as its own proper supplement? How are the consequences related to the 'bare' thing? To the 'bare' and the 'remainder' about which we just spoke? And yet, in another sense, we called them 'nude' just now, we saw them completely naked. Is it by chance that the clothing 'metaphor' comes so easily to Heidegger in speaking of the 'pure and simple' thing? 'The "mere" ("*bloss*"), after all, means the removal (*Entblössung*) of the character of usefulness (*Dienlichkeit*) and of being made. The bare thing (*blosse Ding*) is a sort of product (*Zeug*), albeit a product undressed (*entkleidete*) of its being-as-product. Thing-being then consists in what is then left over. But this remnant (*Rest*) is not actually defined in its ontological character. It remains doubtful (*Es bleibt fräglich*) whether the thingly character comes to view at all in the process (*auf dem Weg*) of stripping off (*Abzug*) everything equipmental (*alles Zeughaften*). . . .' A stripping off (the being-product) won't restore to us the 'remainder' as 'bare' thing. . . . The remainder is not a mere thing. . . . We need 'to think' the remainder differently . . ." ("Restitutions," trans. John Leavey, in *Research in Phenomenology*, 8, 1978, pp. 34–35). As paregonal "remains," the introduction and preface must be conceived to be other than merely hors d'oeuvres. They must be considered ("mourned") as the work of art. See "The Parergon," trans. Craig Owens, in *October* 9, 1979).

* * *

8

JOHN P. LEAVEY

) 7
reconsiderations (

According to the circumstances, Hyppolite is right. The preface is always outside the work, an hors d'oeuvre written, however, after the text, not before. The introduction, on the other hand, is always within, a part of, the system, the work, the book, the logic. Yet Hyppolite revalues the *preface*: "In my opinion Hegel's greatest moment is the point of oscillation between the architecture of the *Logic* and the common consciousness of the *Phenomenology*" ("The Structure of Philosophic Language According to the 'Preface' to Hegel's *Phenomenology of the Mind*," in *The Structuralist Controversy*, Johns Hopkins, 1972, p. 168). The Preface (to the *Phenomenology*) is this point of oscillation.

Derrida follows suit. He reworks the *introduction*, philosophically, logically. In this reworking, the introduction loses its systematic, logical, that is, introductory, character: the "only legitimate place for the Introduction, in this system, is the opening or overture of a *particular philosophical* science, for example the Aesthetics or the History of Philosophy. The Introduction articulates the determined generality of this derived and dependent discourse onto the absolute and unconditioned generality of logic" (*Dissémination*, p. 24), but does so from its place as *overture*. No longer is the introduction "an integral part of the book"; it is an outside opening onto the particular, not the general (logic).

So the preface, first outside the text, becomes most interior to the text. And the introduction, first within the text, a part of it, becomes its exterior. The preface is the exterior becom-

9

ing interior—circumstantially. The introduction is the interior becoming exterior—logically. In other words, the preface becomes introduction, the introduction becomes preface. But both do so only under erasure and in the space of the outside text, the *hors-texte*.

) 8
erasing (

"I have attempted to describe and explain how writing structurally carried (counted-discounted) within itself the process of its effacement and cancellation, all the while marking the *remains* of this effacement, by means of a logic which would be very hard to summarize here" ("Positions," p. 36 [modified]).

Erasure is: deconstruction, writing, inversion and displacement, paleonymy, the science of old names, the double science. (Spivak exposes erasure throughout her preface. She establishes that misunderstanding erasure is misunderstanding Derrida. See her Note 13, p. 318, in *Of Grammatology*. For a specific discussion of an early working of this erasure, see the Translator's Preface to *Edmund Husserl's "Origin of Geometry": An Introduction*.)

In practice, deconstruction is reducible to Derrida's texts, his writing. In other words, deconstruction is *nothing but* writing—writing (and reading), rewriting (and rereading) *"in a certain way"* ("Structure, Sign, and Play in the Discourse of the Human Sciences," in *Writing and Difference,* trans. Alan Bass, Chicago, 1978, p. 288). Derrida's erasing-erased writing—his palimpsest—is the reinscription that continually displaces the reversed hierarchies of metaphysics. (This reinscription seems less evident in Derrida's early discussions of deconstruction than is now the case.) As the intervening tool of reinscription, erasure affords communication. Words, terms, concepts, predicates, logics, metaphysics, literatures are displaced, rewritten, reread. The old name communicates (heterogeneously) through the smudges and the strikes of Derrida's erasure and effacement, his disfiguring or *smearing*.

At the least, erasure *(la rature)* as smearing *(la salissure)* indicates a detour into painting. Into the painting of Cy Twombly and into Roland Barthes's initiation into Twombly's event.

In "The Wisdom of Art," the text for the Catalogue of the recent Twombly exhibition at the Whitney Museum of American Art (10 April-10 June 1979), Roland Barthes talks of the reversal at work in Twombly's art. "In Twombly, another development occurs . . . reversing the usual relationship in classical technique, one might say that strokes, hatching, forms, in short the graphic events, are what allow the sheet of paper or the canvas to exist, to signify, to be possessed of pleasure. . . . Twombly's art—and in this consist its ethic and its great historical singularity—*does not grasp at anything* [ne veut rien saisir] . . ." (trans. Annette Lavers, in *Cy Twombly: Paintings and Drawings 1954-1977*, Whitney Museum, 1979, p. 22).

More specifically, Barthes isolates the *smearing* of Twombly's erasing *(effacer)*:

11

> *Smearing*. This is the name I give to the marks in paint or
> pencil, often even in a material which cannot be specified,
> with which Twombly seems to cover other strokes, as if he
> wanted to erase the latter without really wanting it, since
> these strokes remain faintly visible under the layer which
> covers them. This is a subtle dialectic: the artist pretends to
> have "bungled" a part of his canvas and to wish to erase it.
> But he again bungles the rubbing out and these two failures
> superimposed on each other produce a kind of palimpsest:
> they give the canvas the depth of a sky in which light clouds
> pass in front of each other without blotting each other out.
> . . . (Ibid., pp. 10–11).

Then the surprise of writing itself: "We must count as such
surprises all the interventions of writing in the field of the
canvas: any time Twombly uses a graphic sign, there is a jolt,
an unsettling of the naturalness of painting." And finally the
"clumsiness" of the hand:

> [T]here is . . . the constant "clumsiness" of the hand. The
> letter, in Twombly, is the very opposite of an ornamental or
> printed letter; it is drawn, it seems, without care; and yet, it is
> not really childlike for the child tries diligently, presses hard
> on the paper, rounds off the corners, puts out his tongue in
> his efforts. He works hard in order to catch up with the code
> of the adults, and Twombly gets away from it; he spaces
> things out, he lets them trail behind; it looks as if his hand
> was levitating, the word looks as if it had been written with
> the fingertips, not out of disgust or boredom, but in virtue of
> a fancy which disappoints what is expected from the "fine
> hand" of a painter: this phrase was used, in the seventeenth
> century, about the copyist who had a fine handwriting. *And
> who could write better than a painter?* (Ibid., p. 18; my em-
> phasis)

Texts as canvases, canvases as texts. Derrida's texts and
Twombly's canvases. Twombly's painting and Derrida's writing. Derrida's painting and Twombly's writing. Each illus-

trates the other. For who can paint better than a writer?

Derrida reverses the classical technique, writes "clumsily," smears "clumsily," and leaves the remains for examination, for repetition according to "a logic which would be very hard to summarize here." The "clumsiness" of Derrida constitutes his inimitability: "This 'clumsiness' of the writing (which is, however, inimitable: try to imitate it) . . ." (ibid.). So erasure as smearing offsets the repetition of deconstruction. "Re"-marking the canvases of Derrida as "his own" (not as the restitution or restoration of ownership or truth, but as the inimitable effect of Derrida), smearing "traps" deconstruction in the inimitability of its repetition. Smearing seduces deconstruction into thinking it is repeatable, then deviates its repetition from identity (the ever-repeatable, always re-petitious, tautological, autistic self-enclosure) to a different sameness (the friable, broken into, spaced, scattered, cracked identity). So smearing splits repetition through seduction, deviates repetition from itself, thus revealing its seduction as a false (but necessary) lead.

The false lead. Like Twombly, Derrida "*does not grasp at anything*." His smearing traps without grasping, traps without catching, in the hollowness, the emptiness of its snare. The stroke of "pretense" in writing confirms this. Smearing introduces the *pretended* erasure: "he wanted . . . without really wanting," "the artist pretends," "in virtue of a fancy." But smearing also introduces a *double* pretense: "*as if* he wanted . . . without really wanting," "*as if* . . . in virtue of a fancy." The imprint of fiction is the second (but always already before the first) step (into its own trapless trap) of writing into painting, of painting into writing, of writing into writing, of painting into painting ("The beyond everything, another name for the text insofar as it withstands ontology

13

. . . is not a *primum movens*. It imparts to everything . . . a movement of fiction."—*Dissémination*, p. 65).

An exemplary example of the double pretense is the *parergon*:

What is a title? And what if *parergon* was the title? Here the *faux titre* is art.

(*La Vérité*, p. 22)

The fiction of the frame, here materially presented, establishes the "pretense" for the *faux titre*: the bastard title, falsehood itself, the sham, as well as the half-title of a book. So "art" is the half-title of "Le Parergon." But the false, "bastard" title (falsehood itself) constitutes art as well. The frame's pretense, the *as if* movement of the false lead, imparts fictional imbalance to the *faux titre*. The hollow, open-angled frame of the *parergon* cracks open yet confines within fiction the fiction of *here the faux titre is art*. In short, the frame enchases the fiction of painting into writing, and vice versa. Thus smearing (that is, deconstruction of a sort) takes place only within the frame of the *parergon*. In other words, the smeared-smearing of fiction is fictionalized by fiction itself: Twombly undecides Derrida, Derrida undecides Twombly. Both work only within and without, neither within nor without (that is, *on* the *parerga* which destroy inside and out of) the *faux titre*, that undecidable truth and fiction of every erased stroke, title, word, writing, text, etc.

* * *

(Writing, even erased writing in painting and teaching, is a political act, leaves political remains, establishes political positions. In other words, there is given (*il y a, es gibt*) a politics of deconstruction. Derrida explores this in *La Vérité en peinture*: "According to the consequences of its logic, deconstruction not only attacks the internal building (at once semantic and formal) of philosophemes, but also what would be wrongly assigned as that building's external lodgings, the extrinsic conditions for its performance: the historical forms of its pedagogy; the social, economic, or political structures of this pedagogical institution. Since it tampers with solid structures, 'material' institutions—and not just signifying discourses or representations, deconstruction is always distinguishable from an analysis or "criticism' " (pp. 23–24). And in "Où commence et comment finit un corps enseignant" (in *Politiques de la philosophie*, ed. Grisoni, Grasset, 1976). Finally, see Derrida's two interviews in *Digraphe*, Nos. 8 and 11: "Entre crochets" and "Ja, ou le faux-bond.")

* * *

15

) 9
the erased intro (

You have already remarked that this alleged Introduction prohibited itself from saying in short anything about the *Essay*, about what we would want to find there as its own proper and ventral content. An introduction should not intrude . . . it should not enter into the text, above all not saturate the text with reading. To introduce is to seduce. To seduce the text of course and not the reader, to deviate the text from itself, but just enough to surprise it again very close to its content, which can always open out as nothing: as a central void, an alarming superficiality, a rigorous "abyss." Because of that, to busy ourselves round about: lines, grating, borders, ribs, architecture, after-cuts. . . .(p.108 below)

In place of an introduction. . . . (p. 118 below)

An introduction seduces, sets up the false lead. At least an "alleged" introduction by Derrida. For here "alleged" underscores the reworked (rewritten) introduction—its smeared status, its deconstruction. So erasure once again extends to, mars the act of deconstructing itself: the disfigurement marks not only the term itself, but the "idea" or "concept" as well.

* * *

(Just as there seems to be no inside to the text here— "a central void, an alarming superficiality, a rigorous 'abyss' "—Derrida has said there is no outside either: "*il n'y a pas de hors texte*" (*Grammatology*, p. 158). The text is internally and externally unstable, a situation the introduction seizes upon in order "to deviate the text from itself, but just enough," since *the text does not exist, means nothing, intends nothing.* Thought, too, and perception

16

have a problematic existence for Derrida ("To exist is to be, to be an entity, a being-present, *to on.*" — *Grammatology*, p. 167).)

* * *

) 10
seductions, deviations (

Metaphysics: Condillac's paleonymic handling of metaphysics allows Derrida to isolate the *ana-logic* which fissures Condillac's *Essay*. (In her translation of *Fors* in the *Georgia Review*, Barbara Johnson notes concerning the prefix *ana-*: "*Ana-* indicates: 1) upward, 2) according to, 3) back, 4) backward, reversed, 5) again . . . thus a process of problematizing . . . in an undetermined way" (p. 66n). Reading back from *Fors*, we see *analogic* would be the problematizing of logic in an undetermined way, or at least in an analogical way to *Fors*.) For Condillac, metaphysics is an old name retained in order to communicate, although the "content" of the old name is changed: "The new metaphysics will be called metaphysics only by *analogy* . . . and will be properly named *analysis*, or analytic method. By retracing the true generation of knowledge, by going back to the principles, an actually inaugural practice of analysis can finally dissolve, destroy, decompose the first first philosophy. That means, in the end: *replace the first first philosophy while inheriting its name*" (pp. 35–36 below, my emphasis). Analogy, the ana-logic of paleonymy, reveals and guarantees passage across the gap of

17

sensation and semiotics: the germ of sensation unfolds into a semiotics by analogy, through analysis (p. 46 below).

Genius: To understand the unfolding of sensation into semiotism requires the analogic of genius: *trailblazing (frayage)*. (*Frayage* recalls Derrida's reading of Freud's "scene of writing" from the *Project for a Scientific Psychology* to the "Note on the Mystic Pad," the passage from neuron "facilitation" to the psychic operations of the Mystic Pad.)

* * *

(Note: As translation and development of Freud's *Bahnung, frayage* has been variously translated. Allison prefers the *Standard Edition*'s "facilitation." Mehlman, in the initial translation of "Freud et la scène de l'écriture" for *Yale French Studies*, introduces "fraying," since this word "captures the violence of the movement of this rudimentary form of writing or 'inscription'" (p. 73 of *YFS* No. 48). Bass, in his revised translation of this text (completed before the publication of Spivak's translation of *Of Grammatology*, but not published until two years later in *Writing and Difference*), uses "breaching" to render the term. I have used "trailblazing" in the current text for the single occurrence of this term in order to recall the development of Derrida's previous comments on *la voie frayée*, the marked out trail. Bass, in his use of "breaching," creates a(n) (un)fortunate possibility of confusing *frayage* and *entamer* (first cutting, beginning), since Spivak uses "breach" or "broach" to render *entamer*. In the Husserlian texts by Derrida, Allison and I use "impair" or "undermine" to translate Derrida's seemingly not yet specific use of *entamer*.)

* * *

Trailblazing leads to a new concept of order and generation ("the philosopher must form a new combination of ideas concerning the combination of ideas" — p. 62 below): analogic works through the deviation of *signs*. In other words,

18

although language supports genius, makes it possible, genius adds to language by deviating from "current" usage in order to be original. This deviation constitutes, for Derrida, "the archeology of the frivolous." He explains by citing Condillac:

> "Thus in order to be an original, he is obliged to contribute to the ruin of a language, which a century sooner he would have helped to improve. Though such writers may be criticised, their superior abilities must still command success. The ease there is in copying their defects, soon persuades men of indifferent capacities, that they shall acquire the same degree of reputation. Then begins the reign of subtil and strained conceits, of affected antitheses, of specious paradoxes, of frivolous turns, of far-fetched expressions, of new-fangled words, and in short of the jargon of persons whose understandings have been debauched by bad metaphysics." (p. 67n–68n below)

Imagining: Imagining is the reworking, the reinterpreting (in Freudian terms, the deferred action (*Nachträglichkeit*), a term used as the *faux titre* of the second section of the *Archeology*) of genius's deviation, in order to account for its order. The order of the deviation as deviation is produced and comprehended only after the fact. The most interesting example here is Condillac's own statement within the *Essay* that two pages were misplaced in the text (thus the text and Condillac lacked order) until *after* he had finished writing. Condillac's reworking revealed the lapse of order, the deviation that allowed him, finally and after the fact, to put his writing (and thinking) in order.

* * *

(*Marginal Note*: The translation of *suppléer*. Derrida has frequently and with much insistence discussed *suppléer*. This term has appeared in *La Dissémination*,

19

Speech and Phenomena, and *Of Grammatology*, which contain certain loci classici on this matter. *Writing and Difference* and *La Vérité en peinture* contain other passages as well. The word has generally been translated as supplement, substitute, or supplant (replace). These renderings favor one of the two major senses of *suppléer*: to replace and to complete (*suppléer à* as to make up for). This chain of sense runs throughout the cognates of *suppléer: suppléance, suppléant(e), supplément, supplémentaire*. However, in light of the possibilities given in the *Oxford English Dictionary* (*OED*) and *Webster's Third International*, I have used supply, supplement, and their cognates to translate the family of *suppléer*. Although this translation requires reactivating some obsolete or now rare meanings of supply, it seems in keeping with Derrida's writing. *Supply* (*OED*): "To make up (a whole) by adding something; to fill *up*, complete. . . . To add to (something); to make up a deficiency in; to supplement. . . . To make up for, make good, compensate for (a defect, loss, or void); to compensate for (the absence of something) by providing a substitute. . . . To fulfil, satisfy (a need or want) by furnishing what is wanted. . . . To furnish (a thing) *with* what is necessary or desirable. . . . To fill (another's place); *esp.* (now only) to occupy as a substitute. . . To take the place of; to serve as, or furnish, a substitute for; to make up for the want of; to replace. . . .")

* * *

The sign supplies.

Frivolity: The most frivolous of all styles is the philosophical—that is, the written prose—style. Reading Condillac, Derrida writes: "Philosophical style congenitally leads to frivolity. But the reason for this is logical, epistemological, ontological. If philosophical writing is frivolous, that is because the philosopher cannot fulfill his statements. He knows nothing, he has nothing to say, and he complicates, subtilizes, refines the stylistic effects to mask his ignorance. Thus he misleads, pays change . . . out of the essential emptiness of his discourse. When philosophical writing is difficult, esoteric, reserved to a small number, that is because such writing is hollow" (p. 125 below). However, this frivolity makes deconstruction possible ("Philosophy deviates from itself and gives rise to the blows that will strike it nonetheless from the outside. On this condition alone, at once internal and external, is deconstruction *possible*." — p. 132 below), and the fiction of frivolity makes frivolity itself possible ("What is said by extension is always said improperly" — p. 133 below).

) 11
arch(a)eology: citations (

"...

"—archaeology finds the point of balance of its analysis in *savoir*

"—frivolity defies all archeology, condemns it, we could say, to frivolity

"—archaeology proceeds in the opposite direction: it seeks rather to untie all those knots that historians have patiently tied; it increases differences, blurs the lines of communication, and tries to make it more difficult to pass from one thing to another

"—order, clarity, precision: not only does logic lack these, but writing too—the philosophical style. Philosophical style congenitally leads to frivolity

"—it is nothing more than a rewriting: that is, in the preserved form of exteriority, a regulated transformation of what has already been written. It is not a return to the innermost secret of the origin; it is the systematic description of a discourse-object

"—the root of evil is writing. The frivolous style is the style—that is written

"—this group of elements, formed in a regular manner by a discursive practice, and which are indispensable to the constitution of a science, although they are not necessarily destined to give rise to one, can be called *knowledge*

"—frivolity consists in being satisfied with tokens

"—*du savoir* (trans. A. M. Sheridan Smith, Pantheon, 1972, pp. 183, 170, 140, 182 respectively)

"—*du frivole* (pp. 119, 125, 126, 118 below respectively) . . .""

) 12
parenthesis 2 (

"Derrida, in an *uncharacteristically* positivistic gesture, has settled the question of Lacan's influence upon himself in a long footnote to an interview" (*Grammatology*, p. lxiii; my emphasis). This *uncharacteristic* frame contains the first parenthesis: "(I read while writing: slowly, taking pleasure in prefacing at length each term)." A parenthesis within an uncommon parenthetical gesture underscores the *marginal* (*parergonal*) quality of both parentheses and what comes between. So "deviate the text from itself, *but just enough*": the paregonal difference (the fiction) that erasure inscribes pries open the parentheses, as if to remove the marginality. So deviate the margins, but just enough to communicate. Just enough to produce the frivolous gap making communication possible.

) 13
acknowledgments and notes (

The Archeology of the Frivolous: Reading Condillac has been translated from the first French edition published in Condillac's *Essai sur l'origine des connaissances humaines,* ed. Charles Porset, précédé de *L'Archéologie du frivole* par Jacques Derrida, © Editions Galilée, 1973. This edition has been compared with its 1976 reprinting under separate cover as *L'Archéologie du frivole: Lire Condillac* by Denoël/Gonthier. No significant changes were found.

I would like to thank Robert Hatch and Gregory Ulmer for their helpful suggestions, patient readings, and emendations concerning this text. I must also acknowledge the support of parts of this work by the University of Florida's Humanities Council. Yet I am most indebted to Jacques Derrida himself for his help, support, and friendship.

Finally, I dedicate this work to Arthur Evans.

Gainesville, Florida
September 1979   JOHN P. LEAVEY, JR.

After all, Voltaire is only a man of letters. . . . The true eighteenth-century metaphysician is the abbé de Condillac. . . .[1]

Condillac's most salient qualities are his clearness and precision, a certain analytic force, and with that some finesse and spirit. Considerable flaws are joined to these valuable qualities. Condillac lacks a sense of reality. He knows neither man nor mankind, neither life nor society. Common sense never restrains him. His mind is penetrating but narrow. Headstrong in an excessive love of simplicity, he sacrifices everything for the frivolous benefit of reducing everything to a unique principle. Left without any spirit for observation, he feels more comfortable with word or figure combinations than in faithful and detailed descriptions of facts. From that comes his dry and precise style, of excellent quality but without grandeur, which little by little is credited among us as the true style of philosophy.

[1]Bonnot de Condillac, brother of the famous Mably, was born in Grenoble in 1715, died in 1790. The best edition of his works is that of 1798, in 23 volumes in octavo.

VICTOR COUSIN

Histoire générale de la philosophie

Metaphysics had become insipid. In the very year in which Malebranche and Arnauld, the last great French metaphysicians of the seventeenth century, died, *Helvétius* and *Condillac* were born. . . . Besides the negative refutation of seventeenth-century theology and metaphysics, a *positive, anti-metaphysical* system was required. A book was needed which would systematise and theoretically substantiate the life practice of that time. *Locke's* treatise *An Essay Concerning Humane Understanding* came from across the Channel as if in answer to a call. . . . Is *Locke* perhaps a disciple of *Spinoza?* "Profane" history can answer: Materialism is the *natural-born* son of *Great Britain.* . . . Locke's *immediate* pupil, *Condillac,* who translated him into *French,* at once applied Locke's sensualism against seventeenth-century *metaphysics.* He proved that the French had rightly rejected this metaphysics as a mere botch work of fancy and theological prejudice. . . . It was only by *eclectic* philosophy that Condillac was ousted from the French schools.

KARL MARX

"Critical Battle against French Materialism" [in *The Holy Family,* in *Collected Works,* Vol. 4 (New York: International, 1975)]

1.

The second first —
metaphysics

This book, *An Essay on the Origin of Human Knowledge*, should have opened the doors to a nameless science.

It used to be possible to criticize metaphysics only *as such*. This book does that — which regularly amounts to founding *a* new metaphysics. This book lacks nothing in that respect either — which implies a rigorous and inveterate distinction between *two* metaphysics. We are going to verify this.

"We must distinguish two sorts of metaphysics." For the metaphysics of essences and causes, Condillac very promptly proposes substituting a metaphysics of phenomena and relations ("connections"). For the metaphysics of the hidden, a metaphysics of the open — we could say a phenomenology of the things themselves — and a critical science of limits. One "wants to search into every mystery; into the nature and essence of beings, and the most hidden causes; all these she [metaphysics] promises to discover to her admirers, who are pleased with the flattering idea. The other more reserved, proportions her researches to the weakness of the human understanding [*esprit*] . . . only trying to see things as they in fact are . . ." (*Essay*, Intro., pp. 2–3 [modified]).

Since such a new science was created to give ideas their names, it will consequently have some trouble finding its own name.

What particular name could we assign to a *general* science ending nowhere and utilizing a universal analysis, an analysis that leads us back in all fields of knowledge to the simplest,

most elementary ideas and that also defines their laws of
connection, combination, complication, substitution, repetition? But also—*a problem of principle*—their laws of generation? Will this general theory truly be metaphysics?

Paleonymy: at the beginning of his *Essay*, Condillac seems
very calmly resolved to preserve the old name, provided we
"distinguish two sorts of metaphysics." The opposition of the
two metaphysics, therefore, is analogous to that between the
hidden essence and the proffered phenomenon. In returning to the latter, we reproduce its generation, we "retrace"
(one of the two chief words in the *Essay*) its origin, we go back
there, repeat the origin, and analyze it. Thus, since "good"
metaphysics is the science of origins and true beginnings
(and augurs *La Langue des calculs*: "I begin at the beginning."
"That is why I begin where no one has ever begun before. . . ."), we might feel that "good" metaphysics should
also be presented as first philosophy.

But that is not at all the case! The science of beginnings—
the metaphysics of the simple, of combination and
generation—the new philosophy, will be irreducibly *second*.
Such is its condition.

Long after the *Essay*, Condillac is more prudent and more
uncomfortable than ever about using the word *metaphysics*.
Above all he is anxious to avoid the stumbling-block of
philosophia prote. His metaphysics will not be first philosophy.
Or theology. We must do what Descartes did not succeed in
doing, break with the Aristotelian tradition:

> Perhaps it will seem surprising that I had forgotten to give
> the history of metaphysics, but that is because I do not know
> what this word means. Aristotle, thinking to create a science,
> took it upon himself to gather together all the general and
> abstract ideas, such as being, substance, principles, causes,

relations, and other resemblances. He will consider all these ideas in a preliminary treatise, which he called *first wisdom, first philosophy, theology,* and so on. After him, Theophrastus or some other peripatetic gave the name metaphysics to this collection of abstract ideas. This, then, is metaphysics: a science which proposes to treat everything in general before having observed anything in particular, i.e., to speak about everything before having learned anything: a vain science which bears on nothing and leads to nothing. Since we ourselves raise some particular ideas to general notions, general notions could not be the object of the first science. (*Cours d'études pour l'instruction du Prince de Parme: Histoire moderne*, Book 20, ch. xii, "Des progrès de l'art de raisonner," in *OP*, II, p. 229)

Consequently, the new metaphysics will be second only by returning to the principle's true generation, to its actual production. The new metaphysics will resemble empiricism — without any doubt. But what Condillac denounces in Aristotle's first philosophy is as well an unconscious empiricism, one that takes derived generalities for premises, products for seeds or origins [*germes*]: as a second philosophy incapable of establishing itself as such, it is an irresponsible empiricism. Through a chiasmus effect the new metaphysics, by advancing itself as second philosophy, will methodically reconstitute the generative principles, the primordial production of the general starting from real singularities. The new metaphysics will be called metaphysics. only by *analogy* (it follows that *analogy*, its fundamental operative, will be analogous only to the analogy of the Aristotelian tradition, and here we have the matrix of an infinite set of problems) and will be properly named *analysis*, or analytic method. By retracing the true generation of knowledge, by going back to the principles, an actually inaugural practice of analysis can finally dissolve, destroy, decompose the first first philosophy. That means, in the end: replace the first first philosophy while inheriting its name. Or better still: "supply" it (*suppléer* is the second chief word of the *Essay*).

> Since we need to analyze objects in order to elevate ourselves to true knowledge, it is absolutely necessary to order our ideas by distributing them into different classes and by giving each of them names by which we may be able to recognize them. There lies all the artifice of more or less general notions. If the analyses have been done well, they lead us from discovery to discovery; because, in showing us how we succeeded, they teach us how we can succeed again. The characteristic of analysis is to lead us by the simplest and shortest means. This analysis is not one science separated from the others. It belongs to all the sciences, it is their true method, their soul. I will call this analysis metaphysics, provided you do not confuse it with the first science of Aristotle. (Ibid.)

We need to pursue promptly this *division* of metaphysics. Undertaken from the first page of the *Essay*, this division nevertheless continually complicates the *Essay*'s space and operation.

On the one hand, in fact, "bad" metaphysics has consisted of bad linguistic use coupled with a bad philosophy of language. This "bad" metaphysics can only be corrected, then, by elaborating another theory of signs and words, by using another language. That is the *Essay*'s constant and most obvious intent. For example: "all this quarter of metaphysics has hitherto lain involved in such obscurity and confusion, that I have been obliged to frame to myself, in some measure, a new language. It was impossible for me to be exact, and at the same time to employ such undeterminate signs as vulgar use has adopted" (*Essay*, I, 2, p. 26). *La Langue des calculs* will develop this very project: the constitution of a rigorously arbitrary, formal, and conventional language. But once again the task of establishing this language's *grammar* amounts to metaphysics properly so called — to metaphysics and not to the algebraists' technique of calculation. The philosophical intent is continually reaffirmed when the question is the handling of language and its rules. We could say, the handling of discourse: "I dwelled a long time on the question that the calculators never imagined to treat, because these questions are metaphysical ones and because the calculators are not metaphysicians. They do not know that algebra is only a language, that this language still has no grammar at all, and that metaphysics alone can give it one" (*La Langue des calculs*, in *OP*, II, p. 429).[1]

But, on the other hand, if good metaphysics must be stated in an absolutely artificial grammar, since metaphysics is the very thing that grammar will have instituted, isn't that in order to guide itself by "another" good metaphysics — this time, the most natural one, that which will have preceded all language in general? Isn't that in order to make amends through language for language's misdeeds, to push artifice to that limit which leads back to nature: "There is the advantage that algebra will have; it will make us speak like nature, and we will believe we have made a great discovery" (ibid., p. 435)? In guiding its extreme formalization by the

---

[1] Just as there are two origins, two metaphysics, and so on, there are two barbarisms, "two sorts of barbarism: one which succeeds enlightened centuries, the other which precedes them; and they do not at all resemble each other. Both suppose a great ignorance, but a people who have always been barbarian do not have as many vices as a people who become such after having known the luxurious arts [*les arts de luxe*]" (*Cours d'études*: "Introduction à l'étude de l'histoire," in *OP*, II, p. 9).

necessity of the simple, the language of calculus must reconstitute metaphysics's prelinguistic and natural base. Good metaphysics *will have been* natural and mute: in the end — physics. "Good metaphysics began before languages; and the latter owe to the former the best things they possess. But those metaphysics were at first less a science than an instinct. It was nature that led men without their knowledge, and metaphysics have only become a science, when they ceased to be good and rational" (*Logic,* p. 63).

Science must *cure*, in the transitive and the intransitive senses of this word. Science must cure — (must be cured of) science. Consequently — another displacement and reinscription of duality — there will again be two metaphysics in the very heart of the new science. Once more use will have to distinguish between two metaphysics within the metaphysics Condillac intends to elaborate. Renouncing knowledge of essences and causes and bent back onto the experience of ideas (i.e., effects), the new "metaphysics" (whose "sole object is the human mind [*esprit*]") will articulate in itself these two metaphysics: not the good and the bad, this time, but the good in the form of the "prelinguistic" origin, "instinct," or "feeling," and the good in the form of the highest linguistic elaboration, new language, and "reflection." *De l'art de raisonner* organizes this double system; it gives the rule which must relate to each other the metaphysics of natural instinct and metaphysics as such, the second science which cures.

Metaphysics as such must *develop* and not degrade the metaphysics of natural instinct; metaphysics as such must even reproduce *within* language the relation it has, as language, to what precedes all language. In the order of the human mind, the values of *feeling* and *reflection* define the

38

law of this relation. The first comes to the second in this statement:

> When its sole object is the human mind, metaphysics can be distinguished into two kinds: the one, reflection; the other, feeling. The first disentangles all our faculties. It sees their principle and their generation and accordingly dictates rules to direct them: reflection is acquired by force of study. The second feels our faculties; obeys their action; follows principles which it does not know; is acquired without appearing to be acquired, because fortuitous circumstances have made it natural; is the lot of just minds; is, so to speak, their instinct. Thus the metaphysics of reflection is only a theory which develops, in its principle and its effects, everything that the metaphysics of feeling practices. For example, the latter creates languages, the former explains their system: the one forms orators and poets; the other gives the theory of eloquence and of poetry. (*Cours d'études: De l'art de raisonner*, in *OP*, I, pp. 619–20)

This will have been remarked: although these two metaphysics oppose each other, they succeed one another and develop like practice and theory. The primacy of the practical instance [*instance*] is the most decisive and invariable trait of this new critical metaphysics. But it will resemble less a philosophy of *praxis* than a metaphysics of *fact*.

The first consequence for the *Essay*: since this general theory is no longer a first science or a preliminary method, and in order to take into account and reap the consequences of the development or the acquisition of knowledge, the general theory comes *after* the development or acquisition of knowledge ("in showing us how we succeeded, they teach us how we can succeed again"). The general theory *succeeds* some particular history of science. De facto and de jure, it presupposes the scientific *fact* (as we are going to see), just as the general idea is constructed starting from particular ideas.

Like the theoretical, the general is always engendered. To submit both to analysis is to return to the practical conditions for emergence and to the genetic processes of their constitution. This is not only to decompose a combination into simple elements, to separate the particles of a calculus, but also, by the same movement (yet will it be the same?), to retrace a genesis and reactivate a chain of psychic operations. Would the *Essay* thus be a treatise of practical *psychology*?

But like metaphysics, the word psychology is also outside usage, outside good use, of course: "Even this metaphysics is not the first science. For will it be possible to analyze clearly all our ideas, if we do not know what they are and how they are formed? Before all, then, we must know their origin and generation. But the science attending to this object still has no name, as it is younger. I would call it psychology, if I knew any good work under this title" (*Cours d'études: Histoire moderne*, in *OP*, II, p. 229).

Attentive to becoming, more precisely to "progress," Condillac is always interested in the conditions of the historical possibility of his undertaking. Truly, this historic reflection never lets itself be separated from the undertaking itself; it analyzes some particular conditions and situations but only in order to have posited first the general law of historicity. If philosophy — theoretical metaphysics, the general method — is essentially historical, that is because it always comes *after* the practice of cognition, *after* the upshot or the discovery of a science. Philosophy is always late with respect to an operation of cognition and its occurrence [*fait*].

Thus the general method proposed by Condillac — and so, already, his concept of method, the generalization of the rule after the fact [*après coup*] — can be established only after a discovery — or stroke [*coup*] of genius (a value we will determine farther on). In the philosophic order, this discovery already transposes a discovery, a scientific stroke of genius.

So the *Essay* is engaged on a trail marked out by Locke and Newton. And it draws its lesson from this fact by generalizing the concept of method. "I cannot help thinking, but that a method which has conducted us to one truth may lead us to a second, and that the best must be the same for all sciences. It is therefore sufficient to reflect on the discoveries already made, in order to proceed in the exercise of our inventive powers" (*Essay*, II, 2, §27, p. 318). No doubt Condillac would have subscribed to the words of D'Alembert: by his criticism of innate ideas, his descriptions of the generation and connection of ideas, Locke "created metaphysics, almost as Newton had created physics."[2] Consequently, the content of a method and the concept of method suppose the *marked out trail*. Given the principle of observing nature, the "path of truth is finally opened: it is carved out to the extent that we advance further. . . . Of all philosophers, Newton is certainly the one who knew this route the best, who traces a series of truths tied to one another" (*Cours d'études: Histoire moderne*, in *OP*, II, p. 221). The great principle of analogy authorizes the same statement in the order of human studies [*la science de l'esprit*]:

> Just as we have formed good grammars or poetics only after having had good writers in prose and verse, it happened that we have known the art of reasoning only to the extent that we have good minds, which have thoroughly reasoned in different genres. Thereby you can judge that this art made its greatest progress in the seventeenth and eighteenth centuries. In fact, the true method is due to these

[2]Jean Le Rond D'Alembert, *Preliminary Discourse to the Encyclopedia of Diderot*, trans. Richard N. Schwab (New York: Bobbs-Merrill, 1963), p. 83.

two centuries. It was first known in the sciences, wherein ideas are naturally formed and determined almost without difficulty. Mathematics is the proof of this. . . . If some Tartars wanted to create a poetics, you think indeed that it would be bad because they have no good poets. The same goes for the various logics created before the seventeenth century. Then there was only one way to learn to reason: it was to consider the origin and the progress of the sciences. After the discoveries already made, it was necessary to find the means to make new ones; and to learn, by observing human mental aberrations, not to be engaged in the routes which lead to error. (Ibid., pp. 229–30)

Since method is "first known in the sciences," the philosopher who marks out a trail is the one who repeats (by generalizing) the fact of an earlier rupture, which both transposes and extends that fact. Thus Locke inaugurates —but *after* Bacon and Newton.

Condillac inaugurates *after* Locke.

Before Locke, philosophers and scientists did not recognize Bacon—a lapse of genius, which also *means*, as we will see, by reason of their historical situation.

They should have studied Bacon. This latter philosopher regretted that nobody had yet undertaken to efface all our ideas and to engrave more exact ones on human understanding. [. . .] Locke no longer gave way to any similar regrets. Convinced that the mind can only be known through observation, he himself opened and marked out a route which had not been frequented before him. While considering the progress the sciences of his time owed to experience and observation, he could form this plan and try to execute it. But to his credit his discoveries were not prepared by any of those who had written before him on human understanding. (Ibid., p. 233)

For the moment let us leave to one side the criticisms that Condillac will also direct to Locke. We will consider Locke our model, since Condillac so often invites us to do so. How could Locke carve out a trail while contenting himself to develop, indeed repeat, an earlier rupture? This question forms the paradigm of a much more general set of problems, which can be dug out (with little transposition) of each page of the *Essay*. Trying to answer this question involves interpreting the whole.

If Locke opened a trail by recommencing an operation, it is undoubtedly because he applied a general law to a particular domain. Better still, he discovered, produced, and recognized this field for the first time: that of human understanding. The operation of transposition and of application to which he devoted himself was at the same time productive or constitutive. By proceeding analogically, he discovered an unknown. Invention by analogy, perhaps, is the most general formula of this logic. What is true of analogy (analogy in general or the mathematical analogy of proportion) is also true of analysis. New "objects" are constituted by transposing or proportioning, as well as analyzing, a given. That is why the progress of science, the enrichment of knowledge, can always proceed—as Condillac unrelentingly affirms—by "identical propositions," by analytical judgments.

Under these conditions, Condillac's relation to Locke will be analogous to Locke's relation to his predecessors. The science of human understanding, as properly inaugurated by Locke, is repeated, corrected, and completed by Condillac—particularly concerning the decisive question of language. But he will do nothing less than found it: finally and for the first time. For we must not forget that the *Essay on the Origin of Human Knowledge* concerns itself with [*garde*] a very narrowly delimited object: not even the human spirit, not even the operations of the soul that could as well be

43

related to the will as to the understanding: "The subject of this essay plainly shews that my purpose is to consider [the operations of the soul] only in the relation they bear to the understanding" (*Essay*, I, 2, p. 26).

It is by no means fortuitous that, in the *Logic,* the most explicit text on this matter first concerns analogy, the identical proposition, and the history of science. This text explains the productive functioning of analogy by the principle of a difference of degree ("In analogy we must therefore distinguish different degrees . . ." [*Logic*, p. 89].). In order to understand that in Condillac's system *the combinative is an energetics and the taxonomic element a germinal power,* we must continually associate this principle of difference of degree with the economic principle of force, vivacity, or quantity of connection ("according as the combinations vary, there is more or less connexion between the ideas. I may therefore suppose a combination in which the connexion is as great as it possibly can be. . . . But let me consider an object on that side which is most connected with the ideas I am investigating, the whole shall be fully discovered to my view . . ." [*Essay*, II, 2, §39, pp. 327–28].).

> This analogy [concerning the Earth's double revolution] supposes that the same effects have the same causes; a supposition which, being confirmed by new analogies and new observations can no longer be called in question. It is thus that good philosophers conducted their reasonings. If we want to learn to reason like them, the best means is to study the discoveries which have been made from Galileo down to Newton. . . .
>
> It is thus also that we have tried to reason in this work. We have observed nature and learned analysis from it. With this method we studied ourselves; and having discovered, by a

series of identical propositions, that our ideas and faculties are nothing but sensation which takes different forms, we assured ourselves of the origin and generation of both.

We remarked that the unfolding of our ideas and faculties is only operated by the medium of signs, and could not take place without their assistance; that consequently our manner of reasoning can only be rendered complete by correcting the language, and that the whole art amounts to the accurate or perfect formation of the language of every science.

Finally, we proved that the first languages, in their origin, were well formed, because metaphysics which presided over their formation, was not a science as it is in our times, but an instinct given by nature. . . . (*Logic,* pp. 90–91)

From a distance of thirty years, the *Logic* gives the general rule of the *Essay*—after the fact, but, in proportion to this generality, without the slightest alteration. The rule of the "identical proposition," the analytic rule, implies the genealogical return to the simple—and that progressive development can only be done by combining or modifying a material unmodifiable in itself. Here sensation. That is the first material: informed, transformed, combined, associated, it engenders all knowledge. And the whole *Essay* is organized according to this opposition of material and employment ("The sensations therefore, and the operations of the mind [*l'âme*], are the materials of all our knowledge; materials which our reflection employs when it searches throughout some combinations for the relations that the materials contain" [*Essay,* I, 1, §5, pp. 14–15 (modified)].). His theory of understanding is a theory of sensation, of employment, and of information modifying this first material ("it can be concluded that the operations of the understanding are only sensation itself, which is transformed by attention, comparison, judgment, reflection" [*Cours d'études*: "Précis des leçons préliminaires," in *OP*, I, p. 414]).

Thus there would exist a mute first material, an irreducible core of immediate presence to which some secondary modifications supervene, modifications which would enter into combinations, relations, connections, and so on. And yet this metaphysics (we have seen in what sense it was still a metaphysics), this sensationalist metaphysics—this characteristic cannot be refused it—would also be throughout a metaphysics of the sign and a philosophy of language. If we want to read Condillac and not close ourselves off from his text, if we do not want to be immobilized before a grid of constituted and supervenient oppositions, we must accede to its logic, rather to its *analogic*, which develops a sensationalism into a semiotism. This is indeed a development— not an identity from coincidence, but a development through "identical propositions"—for sensation is not only a simple element, but also a *germ*.

This biological, vitalist, or organicist "metaphor" is constant in Condillac. The whole preamble to *De l'art de penser*, to which we are referred, develops the likewise germinal sentence of the book: "The germ of the art of thinking is in our sensations . . ." [in *OP*, I, p. 717]. And the development of this sentence is the analogical description of thought's development, which *resembles* an animal's.

Similarly, in order to explain the division of the *Essay*, Condillac interprets its theory of signs and language as the system of what develops or "employs" the sensible and elementary, material germ, the subject of the first part: "And yet I have thought proper to make this same subject [the theory of language] a considerable part of the following work, as well because it may be viewed in a new and more extensive light, as because I am convinced that the use of signs is the principle which unfolds [*développe*] the germ of all our ideas" (*Essay*, Intro., p. 11 [modified]).

The opposition of germ and development overlaps that of content (material) and form (employment). The principle of analogy, the analogical analytic, assures the passage, the unity, the synthetic power between both terms of this opposition. Our inquiry should bear on this principle. And if the concept of analogy bears the concept of *metaphor*, still nothing will be said, for example, about the germ when qualified as "metaphor." Preliminarily, Condillac's rhetoric and rhetorical philosophy would have to be reconstituted in order to uphold such a proposition. I will try to do that elsewhere.[3]

What obstinately keeps together the generative and the combinative exigencies can seem in Condillac to be a contradiction, indeed a "deficiency," the opening to "epistemological myths." But that appears to be the case only in comparison with an old philosophical opposition which prohibits thinking these two exigencies other than according to the category of exclusion or (speculative) dialectical synthesis. And perhaps the notion of "epistemological myth" is far from amenable to being reduced to that completely negative and unproductive concept of deficiency. What is the status of all the "epistemological myths" in the history of science? Perhaps the maintenance of *both exigencies* resists, in a nondialectical way, the metaphysical opposition of calculus and genesis. And now we need to ask ourselves under what conditions a text can be found (in this perspective, up to a

[3][Here Derrida is referring to a book he once planned to write, entitled *Le Calcul des langues*. He has abandoned the project for now.—Trans.]

certain point, and according to determinable axes) relevant to the irruptions of a scientific modernity (for example, biology, genetics, linguistics, or psychoanalysis), in which neither "author" nor "production" are "contemporaneous": what uproots such a text—but also every other, provided we recognize this division [*coupe*]—both from its author (this is the first condition of this expropriation) and from the all-powerful constraint of a mythic *episteme*.

What the mythic *episteme* implies of the finite code belongs still and solely to the representation that can be given a determined *episteme*. The imaginary of *one episteme* is the terrain and the condition for the upsurging of the general theory of *epistemes* which alone would make the table, the finite code, and taxonomy its determining norm.[4]

---

[4]Here I am referring to Michel Foucault: "There is a simple historical reason for this: Condillac's logic did not allow a science in which the visible and the describable were caught up in a total adequation." And farther on, in order to explain what in effect is not a matter of course, that such an inadequation is an epistemological obstacle: "Condillac never derived a universal logic from the element—whether this element was perceptual, linguistic, or calculable; he never ceased to hesitate between two logics of operations: of genesis and of calculation. . . . But this generalized form of transparence leaves opaque the status of the language that must be its foundation, its justification, and its delicate instrument. Such a deficiency, which also occurs in Condillac's logic, opens up the field to a number of epistemological myths that are destined to mask it" (*The Birth of the Clinic: An Archaeology of Medical Perception*, trans. A. M. Sheridan Smith [New York: Vintage, 1975], pp. 116–17).

Condillac's "hesitation," his oscillation, would thus be an essential and representative trait of the "Classical *episteme*": "Thus, at the two extremities of the Classical *episteme*, we have a *mathesis* as the science of calculable order and a *genesis* as the analysis of the constitution of orders on the basis of empirical series. . . . Between the *mathesis* and the *genesis* there extends the region of signs—of signs that span the whole domain of empirical representation, but never extend beyond it. Hedged in by calculus and genesis, we have the area of the *table*" (*The Order of Things: An Archaeology of the Human Sciences*, n. trans. [New York: Vintage, 1970], p. 73).

In a remarkable study, "Analyse et genèse: Regards sur la théorie du devenir de l'entendement au XVIII siècle," Jean Mosconi also analyzes the concurrent opposition of the "biological" and the "analytical" models in Condillac's "formula-

What, given a classic metaphysical grid (which Condillac undoubtedly must also reckon with), is debated, even up to the point of not being able to ascertain any categorical overhang; what will be perceived as an internal opposition, contradiction, or deficiency, or as the impotent hesitation between two models (for example, the algebraic and the biological)—indeed, to us, today, this seems to constitute the force and interest of such a text.

That Condillac "himself" had not *laid down* the rule of this debate is no doubt not insignificant, and we must take it into account.

At least we must take into consideration some of the effects this can have in his text and its history.

But provided we know how to limit consequentially the authority of an "author" over his very "own" *corpus*, what works (over) such a text, for all that, ought not be misjudged: a traditional opposition, to be sure (and even older than a so-called Classical *"episteme"*), but also a lever of disorganization.

The lever works at ruining this alternative between genesis and calculus, at ruining the whole system with which the alternative is interrelated—but not in just any way. On the contrary, this lever works with a disconcerting regularity which, without a doubt, can give itself to be read only after the fact—and in a determined situation.

---

tions" (in *Cahiers Pour l'Analyse: Lévi-Strauss dans le XVIIIᵉ Siècle*, No. 4 [1966], pp. 59 ff.). Also see Roger Lefèvre, *Condillac ou la joie de vivre* (Paris: Seghers, 1966): "Condillac's work oscillates and searches for an accord between a concrete empiricism which digs through reality and an abstract logicism which manipulates notions. But the experienced and the thought, the sensible and the intelligible, existence and system, do they let themselves be assimilated?" (p. 83). And: Georges Le Roy's whole "Introduction à l'oeuvre philosophique de Condillac," in *OP*, I, pp. vi–xxxv.

2.

Genius's deferred action [l'après-coup]

To dissolve the alternative opposition: that is a motif which, defining the system's working (that on which it works as much as what works on it), undoubtedly has not been able to find the literal rule of its statement. This explains, at least in part, the disposability, if not the vulnerability, the openness of a corpus exposed to historical blows, to those violent and self-serving operations that are innocently termed lapses in reading.

Of course, the most remarkable example of this is the interpretation of Maine de Biran.

It forms a kind of routine.

Once the debt is recognized, and it was immense, Biran rejects both materialist, determinist sensationalism (the insistence on the simple passivity and the unique principle of experience) and idealism, which is also an abstract algebraism.

The grid of this reading will be very useful.

Handling it becomes even easier when Condillac's "contradictions" or "hesitations" can be adjusted to states or stages in the development, as is said, of his thought. Doing so, Maine de Biran meanwhile completely reserves for himself two possible readings of contradiction: sometimes it is a matter of systematic incoherence, sometimes of historic succession. "Thus his doctrine was not uniform" (*De la décomposition de la pensée*, in *OMB*, III, p. 99). From this statement Biran draws two kinds of conclusions, simultaneously or alternately. On the one hand, Condillac has left us a bad system, a double system ("his doctrine is double," "Condillac's double theory")—an unusual argument on the part of a philosopher who has made duplicity a theme and a norm of his own discourse, who relentlessly sets the structure of the double root and of *homo duplex* over against every "alchemy" of the unique principle. According to Biran, the system can be corrected, can be made more homogeneous and simpler only after Condillac. "Thus his doctrine was not uniform; but it remained susceptible of a new simplification and admitted a more perfect homogeneity. Such is the end that one of Condillac's most famous disciples has proposed since then. . . ." (This concerns Tracy whom, it must be added, Biran criticizes immediately afterwards.)

On the other hand, however, Condillac himself would have parceled out or reduced, from one stage to the other, from one book to the other, the systematic contradiction. Thus this contradiction is no more than historical slippage [*décalage*]—which also is not ordered as simple progress. The systematic vice (which still remains) can provoke relapses or can manifest, at the end of the account, its true constraint. All this is stated in a note:

> While composing the *Traité des systèmes*, Condillac was struck, above all, with the danger that abstractions had to be realized, since that is where he found the common source of all metaphysicians' aberrations. This is also probably what led him to try out a new theory, wherein he could separate the supposed abstract idea of a substantial *ego* (distinct from its accidental modifications) and that of a cause (or productive force internal or external to the same modifications). Expressing in that way only passive effects or modes and transforming the literal [*propre*] idea of faculties, he could also dispense with *reflection*, which, following Locke, he had admitted in his first work as a *specific source of ideas*. Thus did

he compose the *Treatise on the Sensations*. . . . The success of his attempt, the clarity and the precision that it seemed to carry with it in the theory of intellectual faculties—all these strongly predisposed him in favor of an exclusive application of his new method. Now since this method consisted uniquely in forming *a language* (see the first chapter of *Treatise on the Sensations*), i.e., in expressing (and consequently deducing) precisely the simple or compound results of his hypotheses or conventions, he was more and more inclined to believe that it was all there, whatever besides was the object of a science. That is also the degree of simplicity to which he finally brought his doctrine, as can be judged from the *language of calculus*. (Ibid., p. 91, n. 1)

It has often been noted that Condillac had never systematized all his doctrine. In fact, it is very easy, when the various works of this philosopher have been read and compared with the attention they merit, it is easy, I say, to notice that his doctrine is double. And as a result, he presents two completely different systems of philosophy, wherein everything which rallies to the doctrine of the *Treatise on the Sensations* cannot be reconciled with the principles of the *Essai sur l'origine de nos connaissances* [sic]. Indeed, it would be proper to mark all the points where this division occurs, as well as to make an exact abstract of all the important changes the author brought to bear since then on his *Treatise on the Sensations*. Perhaps there we would recognize the need such a brilliant mind felt to give more to the activity of *sentient* and *motor* being, which at first he had considered exclusively under nothing but a single one of its relations to the other. (Ibid., p. 99, n.1)[5]

But everything that would drive Condillac from the simple principle of passive sensibility—his progress, according to

---

[5]The need for a "critical examination of Condillac's double theory" was also posited in the first version of *Mémoire sur la décomposition de la pensée* (cited by Henri Gouhier in his *Les Conversions de Maine de Biran* [Paris: J. Vrin, 1948], pp. 70–71, n. 5).

Biran, starting from the *Essay*—would unfortunately push him toward semiological activism, algebraic artificialism, linguistic formalization. The system is such that no progress is possible for it; its central deficiency will always make it hesitate between two lapses. The model of the "modern" reading is fixed: within another historico-theoretical configuration. This affords thought.

Such would be, will have been, for Biran, the ultimate truth of Condillac's enterprise, just as its end—*La Langue des calculs*—opened the way for him:

> I confess that I have long been searching in vain for the word for this enigma of *transformed sensation*; and that the decomposition of the faculty of thinking, likened to that of an equation (see *Logic*, Part I, ch. vii, and Part II, ch. viii), has often tired my mind. . . . I never thought I held the key to this theory until I had read *La Langue des calculs* and meditated on the foundation of an assertion like the following: everything is reduced to language and its transformations, whatever the object of reasoning, and so on. . . . Then I understood that our philosophy, since it starts with the supposition of the animated statue and according to this fantastic model forms the ideas that are truly archetypes of diverse faculties, could believe itself authorized to compose and decompose the terms by following its own definitions or transforming its language after them: it seems that *La Langue des calculs* had produced the *Logic* and the *Treatise on the Sensations*. However, I think the case is just the reverse. . . . By composing the *Traité des systèmes*, Condillac must have learned to keep himself more on guard against the danger of realized abstractions. This probably induces him to try out a theory wherein he could set aside even [Biran added in his own hand: the use of the term or of] the idea of an incomprehensible substance endowed, outside of present impressions, with some feeling of itself, with some power or *virtuality*, and so on; wherein he could also dispense with reflection which, following Locke, he had admit-

ted in his first work. The success of Condillac's attempt (and the clarity it had appeared, for him, to shed on the theory of intellectual faculties) must have strongly predisposed him in favor of the sound quality of his method. Now as his method consisted principally (in the *Treatise on the Sensations* or at least in its first chapter) in expressing the simple results of its very own conventions, and to deduce accordingly, he was inclined more and more to think that everything could be reduced to this point, whatever the object of the science.[6]

Once this reading machine is recognized, it is no longer surprising to see it spew out its critical cards, successively or simultaneously, against *too much* or *too little* freedom.

First, the *too much* in the *Notes* of the *Cahier-Journal* on the *Essay*: "Condillac does not give enough, it seems to me, to the physical mechanism of ideas. He seems to suggest that we produce ideas by an act of our will, and to believe that they are not the results of the movement of brain fibers or something similar" [in *OMB*, I, p. 213]. Then, indirectly, in all the renewed questionings of algebraism or artificialism, of the arbitrary in general, of everything that amounts to "constructing science thus with some artificial or logical elements, as algebraic formulas are constructed," to "reasoning as exactly and surely with the signs of metaphysics as with those of algebra. Indeed, Condillac seems to have founded nearly all his doctrine on this opinion, to which he shows himself very consistent in his *Treatise on the Sensations,* his *Logic,* and above all his *Langue des calculs*" (*Essai sur les fondements de la psychologie,* in *OMB*, VIII, pp. 166–67; also see *OMB*, III, p. 91).

This criticism of the arbitrary forms a system with the

---

[6]Cited in Gouhier, p. 88, n. 2.

criticism of rationalism, of alchemism (*reduction* to the gold of an abstract, simple, fundamental element), of idealism.[7]

The *too little*: "The way in which Condillac and his school consider these faculties excludes any idea of free activity in them; by subjecting them to any kind of influence whatever from external objects or to the particular *dispositions* of sensibility, they are removed from a mode of culture or of moral development which would tend, as is proper, to free these faculties from their dependence on sensible objects" (*Essai sur les fondements de la psychologie,* in *OMB,* VIII, p. 87, n. 1).[8]

But no more than in Condillac is the question here one of "hesitation," a confused notion which always marks a reading's empiricist limit. Such as Maine de Biran's reading of Condillac, no doubt, but of which we must consequently twice beware.[9]

Customary and insufficiently shaken or disturbed [*sollicitée*], the opposition of activity and passivity forms the hinge. In relying on the evidence of the value of passivity, Biran turns, lets turn the criticism of idealism as an effect of

[7]"Chiefly I am speaking of [Condillac's doctrine] in the *Treatise on the Sensations* . . . which then does not rest on any principle of fact. . . . There he already tacitly and above all presupposed the existence of the personality or *ego*, which preexists in the very nature of the soul or sentient subject, as the alchemists believed" (*Essai sur les fondements de la psychologie*, in *OMB*, VIII, p. 168). "Condillac's doctrine can lead to a kind of idealism wherein the ego would remain alone in the purely subjective world of its very own modifications" (*De la décomposition de la pensée*, in *OMB*, III, p. 137).

[8]Biran began by calling for a "Condillac of the will" who would do for the activity of willing what the *Essay* had done for the understanding: "It would be advantageous to desire a man accustomed to being circumspect to analyze the will, as Condillac has analyzed the understanding" (*Cahier-Journal*, in *OMB*, I, p. 70).

[9]Gabriel Madinier, for example, evokes Maine de Biran's "hesitations." See Madinier's *Conscience et mouvement* (Paris: F. Alcan, 1938), p. 78.

passivity into a criticism of idealism as activism, artificialism, formalism, and so on. This is because the ego remains enclosed in itself only to the extent of its passivity, and too much freedom is the other side of too little freedom: "a kind of idealism wherein the ego would remain alone in the purely subjective world of its very own modifications, while, on the other hand, these modifications (since they are all passive) necessarily presuppose the objective reality of organs which receive them and of bodies which produce them. We cannot, I believe, escape these contradictions without going back to the foundation of a twofold observation, or to the first fact of consciousness and to the primitive condition on which it is founded" [*De la décomposition de la pensée*, in *OMB*, III, pp. 137–38].

Of what does the operation of reading consist, reading which, here for example, amounts to constituting as a formal contradiction, hesitation, or systematic incoherence what, in the other, is claimed or assumed to be duplicity? Why would the couple activity/passivity give rise to a contradiction in Condillac, but to the analysis of a duplicity in Biran? Do rigorous criteria of reading exist to decide this? This question (the relations between textuality on one hand, dialectic and meaning on the other) is specified in this space through that of *repetition*—such would be the economy of the reading proposed here. In Condillac as in Biran (and in the whole textual field indicated by these names), the constant recourse to a value of repetition—whose law and possibility are never questioned—jumbles the opposition activity/passivity, without the rule of this indecision ever coming to conception [*au concept*]. No doubt the limit here is not *a* concept but, with regard to the structure of repetition, *the* concept.

Undoubtedly this simplifying criticism, of which Condillac's philosophy was already the object in the nineteenth century, necessarily bore, simultaneously or alternately, on his materialism *and* his idealism or spiritualism, on his empiricism *and* his formalism, on his sensationalist or geneticist psychologism *and* his logicist algebraism. In France the history of the reading of Condillac is also, according to a relation not at all external or contingent, that of the formation of a University and its models of philosophical teaching. The system of this relation should be analyzed very closely. At the end of a complex and necessary process, Condillac's thought is often limited (in the imagination of so many undergraduates) to a statue's petrified hardheadedness and the evanescence of a rose's scent.

Might Condillac have been surprised? In any case he had no love for the university of his time.[10]

---

[10] A long citation seems indispensable. These texts by Condillac are less available because of the operation to which history has—as it happens—submitted them. Here history is itself represented by the history of the university: "The manner of teaching feels the effects of centuries in which ignorance formed the plan of this way of teaching, for the universities were far from having followed the progress of the academies. If the new philosophy begins to introduce itself there, it is having much difficulty establishing itself; furthermore, it is allowed to enter there only on the condition that it will clothe itself with some scholastic rags. . . . It is not enough to institute good things: we must still destroy the bad ones, or reform them according to the plan of the good ones—according to a better plan, if that is possible. I do not pretend that the manner of teaching is as faulty as in the thirteenth century. The scholastics have curtailed some defects, but imperceptibly and as if in spite of themselves. Left to their routine, they value what they still preserve; and with the same passion they valued what they abandoned. They have given up battles in order to lose nothing: they gave up in order to defend what they have not lost. They do not notice the terrain they have been forced to abandon: they do not foresee that they will be forced to abandon still more. . . . The universities are old and have the flaws of age: I mean they have done little to correct themselves. Can we presume the professors will renounce what they think they know in order to learn what they do not know?" (*Cours d'études: Histoire moderne*, in *OP*, II, pp. 235-36).

Let us consider the *dissolution of the alternative* at the point where it concerns less a determined object or a particular domain than the very project of the science to which it gives rise. Here the question is of a *new* science which, however, would only set in order (by generalizing through analogy) the acquisition of knowledge in order to administer its consequence. Neither a generative model nor a combinative one can, taken separately, account for this *fact*.

The fact that "new combinations" exist. The invention of a science is at once the example and the discovery of this, the production of one of those events and the concept of this law. The *Essay* attributes invention to genius rather than to talent. But let us not pretend to understand what *genius* means. First, we would have to consider *trailblazing* [frayage]: the possibility of a new combination, a creation "in some measure." We are still far from that.

> We do not properly create any ideas; we only combine, by composing and decomposing, those which we receive by the senses. Invention consists in knowing how to make new combinations: there are two kinds of it; talent, and genius.
> Talent combines the ideas of an art, or of a science, in such a manner as is proper to produce those effects, which should naturally be expected from it. Sometimes it requires more imagination, sometimes more analysis. Genius adds to talent the idea in some measure of a creative mind. It invents new arts, or in the same art, new branches equal, and even sometimes superior to those already known. It examines things in a point of view peculiar to itself; it gives birth to a new science; or in those already cultivated it carves out a road to truths, which it never expected to reach. (*Essay*, I, 2, §104, p. 97 [modified])

The concept of *generation*, indispensable to the *Essay*'s structure [*l'édifice*] and to the whole criticism of innatism, is

61

itself a combinative concept, provided novelty is admitted there. The innatist philosophers are blind to this novelty and believe they must choose between the classification of innate ideas and the empiricism of genesis, between calculus and engendering: "The obscurity and confusion which prevails in the writings of philosophers, arises from their not suspecting that there are any ideas which are the workmanship of the mind, or if they suspect it, from an incapacity of discovering their real origin, their generation. . . . Hence, let me beg leave to repeat it, there is a necessity of making a new combination of ideas . . ." (ibid., II, 2, §32, p. 322 [modified]).

As this paragraph from the *Essay* clearly indicates, "a new combination of ideas" designates both a general possibility (new combinations of ideas can be produced) and the concept of this possibility: the philosopher must form a new combination of ideas concerning the combination of ideas. He must produce another concept of the order and the generation of ideas: "Hence, let me beg leave to repeat it, there is a necessity of making a new combination of ideas, beginning with the most simple ideas transmitted by the senses, and framing them into complex notions, which combined in their turn, will be productive of others, and so on."

This lays claim to a new logic: the addition of the new arises from the sole association or complication—analogical connection—of a finite number of simple givens.

As an example of itself, this logic is new, since it is said to belong to a historical configuration breaking with all the past. And yet this logic does nothing but recompose a series of elementary philosophemes belonging to the oldest funds of metaphysics. The example of this logic not only resists the major opposition of continuist or discontinuist, evolutionist or epigeneticist histories (of culture, ideology, philosophy, science), indeed it resists the major option of taxonomy and history. Already capable of these oppositions, more powerful than they (potentially in them [*en puissance d'elles*]), this logic should not be able to become the object of a discipline (traditional or modern and whatever its name) governed by these categories, these criteria of cutting out [*découpage*] and of articulation. This logic thwarts and deconstructs them almost by itself; it is already no longer there when we naively believe we have captured it in a wide-mesh net.

In effect, Condillac not only claims to engender — perhaps we would have to say generate — a new science, or at least bring about a singular contribution to a generation which is one of his "time": he simultaneously proposes a general interpretation, a theory of the general conditions for the upsurge of a theory.

This double gesture, this sort of "historic" reflectivity folds itself over its very own description.

Apparently, everything returns to a theory of genius. The advent of a new science depends on the stroke of genius, and of an individual genius. Genius's essential quality seems to be imagination. But imagination only invents what it must in order to follow nature's dictate and to know which way to begin. This motif is at work from the *Essay* onward (this can be verified), but *La Langue des calculs* strikes its best formulation: "*To invent*, people say, *is to find something new through the force of one's imagination*. This definition is completely wrong." And after he substituted the power of *analysis* for it: "What then is genius? A simple mind who finds what no one knew how to find before it. Nature, which puts all of us on the path of discoveries, seems to watch over it so that it never strays or deviates. Genius begins at the beginning and goes forward from there. That is all its art, a simple art, which for this reason will not be hidden" (*La Langue des calculs,* Book II: "Des opérations du calcul avec les chiffres et avec les lettres," Ch. 1: "L'analogie considérée comme méthode d'invention," in *OP*, II, p. 470). "And, when I say *men of genius*, I do not exclude nature whose favorite disciples they are" (ibid., Intro., p. 420).

What resembles a theoretical decree or a presupposition at once mystical, naturalistic, psychologistic, obscurantistic, and ahistoric, does not limit opening up historical kinds of questions. Such is even a rule of the system of constraints — on these grounds do we retain here the example from this — which binds Condillac's course: the presupposition is put in place in order to set free, as from its own proper limit, the establishment of questions and hypotheses, of inquiries on the conditions of possibility. The concepts of sensibility and experience, which define the field of those possibles and open questioning about origins, are constituted thus starting from an article of faith. ("Whenever therefore I happen to say, *that we have no ideas but what come from the senses*, it must be remembered, that I speak only of the state into which we are fallen by sin. This proposition applied to the soul before the fall, or after its separation from the body, would be absolutely false. I do not treat of the knowledge of the soul in the two extreme states; because I cannot reason but from experience. . . . Our only view must be to consult experience, and to reason only from facts, which no one can call in question" [*Essay*, I, 1, §8, pp. 18–19].)

Thus the genius who "finds what no one knew how to find before it" nevertheless finds only on certain conditions. The origin of one science is not the origin of science itself. The distinctions proposed by the *Dictionnaire des Synonymes* between *find, discover, invent, come or light upon* [*rencontrer*], clearly show that for Condillac a scientific discovery, indeed the institution of a new science, belongs to the complex chain of a history in which fact, hypothesis, concept, theory, and so on, are not homogeneous and contemporaneous "novelties." These definitions take as their example — but it is at one blow more than an example — one of the two discoveries that Condillac will consider (in a sense still to be stated precisely) to be the "models" and the conditions for exercising his own discourse: that of Newton. "In the birth of the arts and sciences, more things are *come upon* than *discovered*. In the last century more was *discovered* than *come upon*. Only by reflecting on what has been *come upon* has one begun to make any *discoveries*. Some individuals before Newton *came upon* the attraction which he discovered and which Descartes could not find" (*Dictionnaire des synonymes,* in *OP*, III, p. 545; also see *La Langue des calculs*, in *OP*, II, p. 471).

The medium of the conditions for discovery is always the history of language, the history of sign systems.

This history, which itself has natural conditions that are analyzed in the *Essay*, always prepares the stroke of genius. This stroke cannot be produced before the constitution of a certain state of language, of certain semiotic possibilities in general. The least natural language, algebra, and the language of calculus, at once science and language, remain *historical* possibilities. They have a history and they open up a history.

> The circumstances favourable to the displaying of genius,
> are always to be come upon in a nation, when the language

begins to have fixed principles and a settled standard: such a period is therefore the epocha of great men. . . .

If we recollect that the habit of the imagination and memory depends intirely on the connexion of ideas, and that the latter is formed by the relation and analogy of signs; we shall be convinced that the less a language abounds in analogous expressions, the less assistance it gives to the memory and the imagination. Therefore it is not at all proper for the exertion or display of talents. It is with languages as with geometrical figures; they give a new insight into things, and dilate the mind in proportion as they are more perfect. Sir Isaac Newton's extraordinary success was due to the choice which had been already made of signs, together with the contrivance of methods of calculation. Had he appeared earlier, he might have been a great man for the age he would have lived in, but he would not have been the admiration of ours. It is the same in every other branch of learning. The success of geniuses who have had the happiness even of the best organization, depends intirely on the progress of the language in regard to the age in which they live; for words answer to geometrical signs, and the manner of using them to methods of calculation. In a language therefore defective in words, or whose construction is not sufficiently easy and convenient, we should meet with the same obstacles as occurred in geometry before the invention of algebra. (*Essay*, II, 1, §§146–47, pp. 287–88 [modified]; also see *Cours d'études: Histoire Moderne*, in *OP*, II, p. 222)

But if genius is borne by language, by a certain state of the analogy of signs, it is also defined by the science of that language and state. This science is a science of combination, and of the "new combination." This science takes into account both a historical development of the analogy of signs and the peculiar genius of language, which is itself only a particular manner of combining: "I would fain know whether it be not natural for every nation to combine their ideas according to their own peculiar genius; and to connect a certain fund of principal ideas with different adventitious notions, according as they are differently affected. Now these combinations authorized by time and custom, are properly what constitutes the genius of a language" (*Essay*, II, 1, §160, p. 298 [modified]).

Yet nothing of all this seems to make history. The word and even more the notion of history seem incompatible with this conception of development, progress, of changes of every kind. The order of nature limits them on every side. Condillac speaks of "this historical account of the progress of language" (ibid., §162, p. 299 [modified]), of "the history of language" (ibid., I, 2, §49, p. 60), of "the history of the human spirit" (*Cours d'études: Histoire moderne*, in *OP*, II, p. 221), but the question concerns history as a narrative retracing a prescribed progress, a natural progress. History is only the development of a natural order. On one hand, certainly, the role of genius is never obliterated. Language furnishes it elementary conditions which it has no more than to recognize in order to bring them into play. But genius keeps in its own right some power that it in turn gives to language: "Though it be true that great men partake, in some sense or other, of the character of their nation, yet they have still something that distinguishes them from the crowd. They see and feel in a manner peculiar to themselves, which they cannot communicate without imagining *new turns of expression within the rules of analogy, or at least so as to deviate from them as little as possible.* Hence they *conform to the genius of their language, to which at the same time they communicate their own" (Essay,* II, 1, §153, p. 292 [modified]; my emphasis).[11]

[11]"So as to deviate from them as little as possible." The archeology of the frivolous is this deviation of genius: "After having shewn the causes of the last improvements of language, it will be proper to inquire into those of its decline: they are indeed the same. . . ." The man "of genius" "tries a new road. But as every style analogous to the character of the language, and to his own, hath been already used by preceding writers, he has nothing left but to deviate from analogy. Thus in order to be an original, he is obliged to contribute to the ruin of a language, which a century sooner he would have helped to improve. Though such writers may be criticised, their superior abilities must still command success. The ease there is in copying their defects, soon persuades men of indifferent capacities, that they shall acquire the same degree of reputation. Then begins the reign of subtil and strained conceits, of affected antitheses, of specious paradoxes, of frivolous turns, of far-fetched expressions, of new-fangled words, and in short of the jargon of persons whose understandings have been debauched by bad metaphysics. The public applauds: frivolous and ridiculous writings, the beings of the day, are surprisingly multiplied . . ." (*Essay,* II, 1, §§158–59, pp. 296–97 [modified]).

3.

Imagining — conceptual stand-in and the novel of force

If there were only (natural or national) genius and the progress of language, we might think there would not be any history. Individual genius, the "new combination," the "new turns of expression within the rules of analogy," and idiomatic deviation, all these make history, so far as history involves the unforeseeable novelty of the event. Conversely, if individual genius, its event, cannot be reduced to its own conditions, we might think there is no more history, only gaps [*écarts*], irruptions, discontinuities referred to a power of singular imagination. But, as we have already seen, invention no more depends on imagination than imagination has the ability to create anything whatever. The fact is, production of the new—and imagination—are only productions: by analogical connection and repetition, they bring to light what, without being there, *will have been* there.

All this leads us back to the time of repetition, to the status of imagination as described in the *Essay*. Imagination is what *retraces*, what produces as reproduction the lost object of perception, the moment attention (of which imagination is nevertheless only the first modification) no longer suffices to make the object of perception *subsist*, the moment the first modification of attention breaks with perception and regulates passing from weak presence to absence. Such is the case [*instance*] of the sign and then of the historic milieu in general, the element of deviation [*écart*] wherein individual genius and the progress of languages are interchanged.

71

Experience shews that the first effect of attention is to make those perceptions which are occasioned by their objects to subsist still in the mind, when those objects are absent. They are preserved, generally speaking, in the same order in which the objects presented them. By this means a chain or connexion is formed amongst them, from whence several operations, as well as reminiscence, derive their origin. The first is imagination, which takes place when a perception, by the force alone of the connexion which attention has established between it and the object, is retraced at the sight of this object. Sometimes, for instance, the bare mentioning of the name of a thing is sufficient to represent it to one's self, as if it were really present. (*Essay*, I, 2, §17, p. 38 [modified])

First let us remark the value of the "force of connection." Condillac does not insist on this, but it is an active spring of all his discourse. The passage (continuity and/or rupture) from one operation or structure to another and the articulation, then, of their concepts always amount to a difference of force, of the quantity of force. But—such is the universal law of analogy which dominates this whole set of problems— quantity of force is always quantity of connection. . . .

Force is first determined as force of connection and its quantity as quantity of connection.

What is a quantity of connection?

Perhaps this question, which Condillac never seems to answer, could guide a deconstructive reading of the *Essay*. The "new" of a combination arises from the analysis of a certain—the greatest—"quantity of connection":

It has been already observed that the analytic method is the only mean or instrument of invention. But some perhaps will ask me, by what mean or instrument are we to discover the analytic method itself? I answer, by the connexion of ideas. When I want to reflect upon an object, in the first place I observe that the ideas I have of it are connected with

those I have not, and which I am in search after. I observe
next, that the one and the other may be combined a great
many ways, and according as the combinations vary, there is
more or less connexion between the ideas. I may therefore
suppose a combination in which the connexion is as great as
it possibly can be; and several others in which the connexion
gradually diminishes, till it ceases to be sensible. If I view an
object on that side which has no sensible connexion with the
ideas I am seeking, I shall find nothing. If the connexion is
superficial, I shall discover very little; my conceptions shall
seem to be no more than the consequence of a violent
application, or even the effect of chance, and a discovery of
this nature will afford me very little assistance towards
making any further progress. But let me consider an object
on that side which is most connected with the ideas I am
investigating, the whole shall be fully discovered to my
view. . . . (*Essay*, II, 2, §39, pp. 327–28 [modified])

The quantity of connection between a known and an
unknown, analysis as the analogical process (eventually of
proportionality), innovation as revelation, the energy connecting the present to the absent, difference of degree as a
structural opposition, discontinuous continuity—all these
increase and articulate themselves in the concept of force as
the force of repetition (retracing, supplying).

In this reading, we can ascertain that the system of this
articulation or this increase regularly produces a silent ex-
plosion of the whole text and introduces a kind of fissure,
rather fission, within each concept as well as each statement.
In the context occupying us here, there are two examples.

1. The explanation gets carried away, disappropriates itself, since it overplays the notion of force whose obscurantist
effect or "metaphoric" value Condillac denounces elsewhere. The metaphoric, hence analogical value: the force of
connection, the analogical energy can, itself, give rise only to
an analogical concept. Here we must refer to the *Dictionnaire*

des synonymes (the natural product of a philosophy of analogy and the application of a metaphoristic theory of language), to the article on *attraction*, the physical model of the universal connection that is transferred by analogy into the realm of ideas:

> ATTRACTION. n.
> Name given to a cause no more known than impulse.
> [It is a force which draws just as impulse is a force which pushes. Now the word *force* is a name given to a cause we do not know at all; see *force*.] *Attraction* is universal and in some cases the laws it follows are known. But my plan does not include dwelling on words of this kind. I only speak of attraction because it is the cause of weight, of gravity, and so on, about which I have been able to create an article. Yet I could predict that this word will be used figuratively when Newton's system will be more generally known. In fact, for example, why wouldn't one say: there is an *attraction* between man, but it acts only at the point of contact, or at most at a small distance. [In *OP*, III]

Now read the article on *force*. Just as everything he did while criticizing this value in the article on *attraction*, Condillac in advance outmaneuvers, captures Biran's object on the flank.[12] The primitive sense proceeds from the internal

---

[12]"There is in us a principle of our actions, which we feel but cannot define. We call it *force*' (*TS*, I, 2, §11, p. 8, n. 1). From this internal feeling, but from it alone at first, derives the *idea* we have of force. For Condillac never denied we have some idea of force, even if this idea does not give rise to a cognition or definition of the object ("We owe to internal feeling or consciousness the first idea of what we call *force*."). Thus it would be necessary at least to complicate Maine de Biran's criticism: "In that case, I ask if we can confuse this capacity or receptive property and its passive results on the one hand, while setting aside, following the example of natural philosophers, the idea of an *active* force, as real in us as the very feeling of our existence" (*De la décomposition de la pensée*, in *OMB*, III, p. 101). "No, undoubtedly we do not at all form *images* of forces; but as to the *idea* or inner feeling of what we exert in an effort, a voluntary movement, how do you deny it?" (ibid., p. 185, n. 1).

feeling of effort and is, like every primitive sense, sensible, physical, of the order of one's own body. This sense is transferred and "figuratively" extended by metaphor and analogy—such is the rule which organizes this whole dictionary of synonyms:

> We owe to internal feeling or consciousness the first idea of what we call *force*. This quality is what makes us able to move and carry our bodies, to overcome what resists us, to resist what acts on us. . . . From the body this word has been transferred to the mind and the soul. . . .*Forces* are taken for the multitude of things of which they are the effect. . . . This word was also transferred to inanimate things. But then it is the name of a cause of which we have no idea and which we know only by effects; indeed this cause has occasioned various verbal disputes among those who thought they had discovered it and consequently caused rather absurd things to be said. See what the natural philosophers [*les physiciens*] have said about the *force* of bodies. . . . In addition, we say the *force* of a thought, an expression, an argument, a discourse; but analogy enlightens us on these examples and on all the others. [*Dictionnaire*, in *OP*, III]

Thus only in the realm of physics, the science of inanimate bodies, is *force* the name of a cause of which we have no idea. But *force* does not recover its primitive sense when passing from inanimate bodies to spiritual animation, to thought, mind, or idea: this last case stills concerns a metaphor ("From the body this word has been transferred to the mind and the soul. . . . In addition, we say the *force* of a thought . . . a discourse; but analogy enlightens us. . . ."). The "first idea," the primitive sense, then, is reserved for one's own internal, bodily experience, to the sensible "internal feeling or consciousness." But here we are short of all definition. Since Condillac refers in the *Essay* to "the force alone of the connexion" to define the relation between a presence and an absence, a perception and all its others; since he refers to beginning with attention and imagination, in what sense must we understand the word *force*? To what sense must we extend it? Reserve it? And if, the organizing thesis of this discourse, language is primordially metaphorical; if the primitive is figured, where is force found? Here we only want to begin considering this question.

2. Another disappropriation, another fission: this tampers with the very concept of what disappropriates, what produces the "new combination," what opens up the given; it tampers then with the whole system which links repetition (retracing-supplying), sign, time, analogy.

It concerns imagination.

First of all, in Chapter II (*Essay*, I, 2, p. 38), imagination is purely *reproductive*, it "retraces" the perceived. In this sense, imagination invents or innovates nothing; it only combines in relation to each other the given's finite presences. But the force connecting the present to the absent sets free production of the "new."

Productive force is also called imagination.

This name will not be equivocal provided we know how to regulate its use; however, it is the name of what (along with analogy, metaphor, the connection of known to unknown, of presence to absence) will introduce into all language the risk of ambiguity.

We can say that all the problems of the *Essay* are spread out between the two senses of the word *imagination*, the reproductive imagination which retraces (connection is in some way tied to this) and the productive imagination which, in order to supply, adds something more. Its *freedom* is defined some chapters farther on and occasions a note:

76

From the power we have of reviving our perceptions in the absence of objects, is derived that of reuniting and connecting the most distant ideas. Every thing is capable of assuming a new form in our imagination. By the freedom with which it transfers the qualities of one subject to another, it unites in one only the perfections which nature would judge sufficient for the embellishment of many. Nothing at first sight seems more contrary to truth, than this manner in which the imagination disposes of our ideas. And indeed if we do not render ourselves masters of this operation, it will infallibly mislead us; whereas if we learn how to subject it to rule, it will prove one of the principal sources of all our knowledge. (*Essay*, I, 2, §75, pp. 78–79 [modified])

The note is called for right here. Before we cite it, let us remark that the freedom is only one of transfer (a displacement of predicates from one subject to another and a metaphorical operation), and that there are not only two concepts of imagination: the productive imagination itself has two possible values or effects: truth and nontruth.

The note:

Hitherto I have taken the imagination for that operation only which revives the perceptions in the absence of objects: but now that I consider the effects of this operation, I find no inconveniency in following the common acceptation; nay, I am obliged to do it. Hence it is that in the present chapter I take the imagination for an operation, which by reviving our ideas, forms new combinations of them at will. Thus the word *imagination* shall henceforward have two different significations with me: but this shall not occasion any equivocation or ambiguity, because the circumstances in which I use it, will determine each time my particular meaning. (Ibid., p. 79)[13]

---

[13]A remarkable index, the imagination appears twice, in two places, under two different titles on the second to last page of the *Essay*: at the same time as material

"If we render ourselves masters of this operation": we can verify that, in the *Essay*, "to render oneself master of," "to dispose of," is the final sense of every operation. If action and the language of action are at the beginning, Condillac always determines them axiomatically as mastery or as the movement toward mastery. With imagination's duplicity functioning as a hinge, to render oneself master of, to control the ambiguity and risks, is the major strategic operation of mastery — we could almost say, mastery itself.

But since mastery, in order to be what it is, must take possession of what is not, of nothing then, to be sure it is never itself. Mastery, *if there is any*, does not exist.

The imagination*s* constitute the place of history and the "progress of language." The narrative we can construct will have to be probable but, in the milieu of imagination, of language on language, always risks *resembling* a fable. Its affinity with the novel or romance, indeed with a mythic epistemology,[14] remains congenital to the narrative.

---

and as employment, as content and as form. "The senses are the source of human knowledge. The different sensations, perception, consciousness, reminiscence, attention and imagination, the two last considered as not yet subject to our controul, are its materials: memory, imagination, as subject to controul, reflexion, and the other operations, employ these materials: the signs to which we are indebted for the habit [*l'exercice*] of these very operations, are the instruments they make use of: and the connexion of ideas is the first spring which puts all the rest into motion" (*Essay*, II, 2, §53, p. 338).

The opposition material/employment thus traverses and divides the concept of imagination which is consequently its element or environment. Correlatively, the opposition which internally marks the imagination is also that of nonmastery to mastery, of *noncontrol* to *control*, of *disposition* to *nondisposition*. This opposition furrows and orders the whole *Essay*. The sign, signification is the operation of mastery, the *putting-under-the-control-of*, at once (as we have just seen) as the condition and the instrument of exercising. If there are two concepts of imagination, there are two concepts or values of the sign, and that will not be without consequence.

[14]"Ignorance always rushes its judgments and treats as impossible everything it does not understand. The history of our faculties and ideas seems a completely

From this historical account of the progress of language every body may see, that to a person well acquainted with languages, they are a painting of the character and genius of every nation. He may see in what manner the imagination first made a combination of ideas from prejudice and passion. . . . But if the manners of a people influenced language, the latter, as soon as its rules were ascertained by celebrated writers, had in its turn an influence on manners, and for a long time preserved to each people their peculiar characteristic.

Some perhaps will look upon this whole history as a romance: but they cannot at least deny its probability. (*Essay*, II, 1, §§162–63, p. 299 [modified])

Voltaire had written on Locke: "Such a multitude of reasoners having written the romance of the soul, a sage at last arose who gave, with an air of the greatest modesty, the history of it."[15] The *Essay* regularly defines Locke's enterprise as a model, but as one to be corrected and completed, still a fable to be made more historical, more probable.

What Newton has accomplished to perfection in the realm of physical science, Locke has only roughed out in the field of psychology.

The *Essay* makes two major references to this. Newton understood the order of truths in the science of the physical universe. But in doing this, he not only gave Condillac an example to transpose, the particular model of a methodical and formal success in a different domain. Condillac now has

---

chimerical romance to minds which lack any penetration: it would be easier to reduce them to silence than to enlighten them. In physics and astronomy, how many discoveries were judged impossible by ignorant people of former times!" (*De l'art de raisonner*, in *OP*, I, p. 633).

[15]*Lettres philosophiques*, 1734 [first published in 1733 in London as *Letters Concerning the English Nation*, tr. John Lockman; selections rpt. and slightly modernized in *The Enlightenment: A Comprehensive Anthology*, ed. Peter Gay (New York: Simon and Schuster, 1973), pp. 147–74; citation found on p. 162—Trans.].

access to a universal content: the idea of a simple and unique principle ruling the connection of things among themselves on the basis of one fundamental property.

What did Newton discover? Condillac explains in *De l'art de raisonner* by advancing a "comparison," a technical comparison to bring into view a physical truth. If the beam of a balance is placed on the tip of a needle, and if the farthest bodies are made to turn around the same center, we will have "the image of the universe." The machine, the balance or lever, is the principle of all other machines, simple (wheel, pulley, inclined plane, pendulum) or compound. "The identity is sensible; the machines take different forms in order to produce more conveniently different effects, but in the beginning they are all only one same machine. Now our universe is only a great balance. . . . [The] point of suspension, fulcrum, and the center of gravity are at bottom the same thing. This comparison is enough for us to make comprehensible how all these masses are regulated in their course by that same force which makes this notebook fall if you stop holding it up. . . . For if there is fundamentally only one machine, there is fundamentally only one property" (in *OP*, I, p. 676).

This unique property assures discourse of the power to proceed by identical propositions, that is, self-evidentially [*dans l'évidence*], since identity is "the only sign of evidence" (ibid., p. 677). "So identity is the sign by which a proposition is recognized as self-evident; and identity is recognized when a proposition can be translated into terms which return to those very terms, *the same is the same*" (ibid., p. 621; also see *Logic*, pp. 86–88).

The principle of evidence which alone "must exclude every kind of doubt" (ibid., pp. 636–37) is the ultimate appeal. Here recourse to the identical (nontautological) proposition follows the rule of the evidence of reason that Condillac distinguished from evidence of fact and evidence of feeling (ibid., p. 620).

In transposing the Newtonian discovery into the psychological order, Condillac also submits the *Essay* to the criterion of evidence and of a non-Cartesian indubitability ("our only aim should be to discover a fundamental experience which no one can question, and will be sufficient to explain all the rest" [*Essay*, Intro., p. 6 (modified)]). In combining and overseeing the three types of evidence, he studies as well the universal connection (of ideas among themselves, of ideas and signs, of signs among themselves in analogy). He leads all experience back to a first property which knows itself and which does nothing then but modify itself: sensibility.

Although the *Essay* only treats the understanding, it implies the later proposition of the *Treatise on the Sensations*: "Judgment, reflexion, desires, passions, etc. are only sensation itself differently transformed" (Dedication, p. xxxi [modified]). The *Essay* states: "The perception or the impression caused in the mind [*l'âme*] by the agitation of the senses, is the first operation of the understanding. The idea of it cannot be acquired by any discourse or words whatsoever; nothing can convey it to us but the reflexion on what passes within us, when we are affected by some extraneous impression on the senses" (I, 2, §1, p. 27).

The general principle of analogy authorizes this transposition of Newtonian discourse. No doubt this principle, like every philosophy of metaphor which proceeds from it, gives rise to an ambiguous axiology. Analogy can also mislead us, but then that is because the analogy is weak, the "quantity of connection" is not great enough. Analogy creates language and method. Analogy makes possible and homogeneous the passage from one place of discourse to another, the transfer of a scientific model into another field. Analogy is itself the unity of method, it is *the* method.

Although Condillac often criticized the mathematism of certain philosophers, he accepts consideration of the mathematical object and method as models, but as models of language included in the general field of science as particular domains. This fundamental homogeneity of the scientific field in general depends not only on discursive analogy but also on the fact that this analogy is natural, forms a sequence with nature. Analogy never does anything but extend natural productions. The continuity of this observation can be verified from the *Essay* to *La Langue des calculs*:

> The first expressions of the language of action are given by nature, since they are a continuation of our organization: the first expressions are given, analogy forms the others and extends this language, which little by little becomes suited to representing our ideas of whatever kind.
>
> Nature, which starts everything, starts the language of articulated sounds, just as it has begun the language of action; and analogy, which completes languages, forms them correctly, if it continues as nature has begun.
>
> Analogy is properly a relation of resemblance: then a thing can be expressed in many ways, since there is nothing which does not resemble many other things.
>
> But different expressions represent the same thing under different relations, and the mental aspects, i.e., the relations under which we consider something, determine the choice we should make. . . .
>
> Languages are all the more imperfect since they seem more arbitrary; but remark that they seem to be less so in good writers. When a thought is well rendered, everything is founded on reason, even up to the placement of each

word. Thus are the men of genius who have made everything that is good in languages; and, when I say *men of genius*,
I do not exclude nature whose favorite disciples they are.

Algebra is a well-made language, and it is the only one:
nothing there appears arbitrary. Analogy, which never gets
away, leads sensibly from expression to expression. Here
usage has no authority. Our concern is not to speak like the
others; we must speak according to the greatest analogy in
order to come to the greatest precision. Those who made
this language have felt that stylistic simplicity makes all its
elegance: a truth less well-known in vulgar languages.

As soon as algebra is a language that analogy constructs,
analogy which forms language forms the methods: or
rather, the method of invention is only analogy itself.

Analogy: that then is what all the art of reasoning is
reduced to, as is all the art of speaking; and in this single
word we see how we can instruct ourselves of others' discoveries and how we can make some of them ourselves. . . .

Mathematics is a well-discussed science, whose language is
algebra. So let us see how analogy makes us speak in this
science, and we will know how it ought to make us speak in
the others. That is what I propose. Thus mathematics,
which I will treat, is in this work an object subordinated to a
much greater object. The question is showing how this
exactitude can be given to all the sciences, an exactitude
believed to be the exclusive lot of mathematics. (*La Langue
des calculs,* in *OP*, II, pp. 419–20)

This situation of mathematics (as model and included
object) results from the unlimited generality of the principle
of analogy: the types of analogy (sensible, natural re-
semblance, proportionality, and so on) are analogous among
themselves (ibid., p. 450). If the end of the *Essay* seems to
criticize philosophical mathematism and even, as is thought,
the mathematical in general, it aims to make them only the
confused transposition of what is the least mathematical:
geometry, the geometer's preference for synthesis

("Geometricians themselves, who of all philosophers ought to be best acquainted with the advantages of the analytic method, give the preference very frequently to the synthetic. Hence it is that when they quit their calculations to enter into researches of a different nature, we find they have neither the same clearness, nor precision, nor the same extent of comprehension. Of four celebrated metaphysicians, Des Cartes, Mallebranche, Leibnitz, and Locke, the latter is the only one that was not a geometrician, and yet how vastly superior is he to the rest!" [*Essay*, II, 2, §52, pp. 337–38].). The program of *La Langue des calculs* is on the other hand very clearly opened (ibid., II, 2, §§7 ff., pp. 304 ff.).

The status of the two models differs. Newton must be transposed, Locke must be completed and corrected.[16] On numerous points, which all seem reducible to this: Locke missed the sign because he lacked order. He did not recognize the principle of the germ's development ("the use of signs is the principle which unfolds the germ of all our ideas" [ibid., Intro., p. 11 (modified)]), because he did not radically analyze the germ or seed.

Lack of order. If there has been historical progress, for example from Locke to Condillac, that is because the natural order had been perverted. If that order had been immediately perceived, there would not have been any historical density. But even more so, not without a return to the natural order. We will have to take these two motifs into account.

---

[16]Besides the criticisms formulated by the *Essay*, see notably the *Extrait raisonné du Traité des sensations* (in *OP*, I, pp. 324 ff.) and *De l'art de penser* (in *OP*, I, pp. 738 ff. and p. 774).

They not only explain Condillac's interpretation of his own relation to Locke's discovery, but also Condillac's lineage in relation to himself; also the "progress" of his own thought: first within the *Essay*, then from the *Essay* to subsequent works, in particular to the *Treatise on the Sensations*. Condillac multiplies the considerations of history in his own discourse. He does not hold them as marginal. They must be part of the discourse itself which, marking out the trail, must be recounted, must explain its steps (if not its faux-pas), the rules it followed or those it should have followed.

That such analyses are part of the principal discourse undoubtedly indicates their importance and seriousness. But simultaneously we are ordered not to trust this too much: these analyses tell us what Condillac was thinking of doing, or rather thought he had done. This ensemble of rules had to constitute method (and the general concept of method) after the fact, as the reflection of a success; a method which should allow successors to repeat the science and multiply its discoveries. The *methodological* operation is in some way a *revolutionary* operation. A rare merit is accorded Descartes, in a passage of the *Essay* which will be, like so many others, literally reproduced by *De l'art de penser* (in *OP*, I, p. 768): "Philosophers would have supplied our general incapacity of self-reflexion, if they had left us the history of the progress of their minds. Des Cartes indeed has done it, and this is one of the great obligations we owe him. . . . I am apt to think that this contrivance greatly contributed to the revolution occasioned by this philosopher" [*Essay*, II, 2, §41, pp. 329–30]. If the *Essay's* "truth," its possibility, then its limits have twice appeared after the fact; if the system is unfolded, *explained* in a history, that is because there was a lack of order, because the natural order of ideas was violated. The retrospective evidence first occurs within the *Essay*, in the course of its exposition.

But this exposition is not the outside of his labor. What, up to the end of the book, will have been hidden by a fault of composition, by a lapse in the order of didactic linking, is precisely the extent of "the principle of the connexion of ideas." This principle is nothing but the principle of order itself, of order conforming to nature. What the lack of order will have hidden—not any particular object or moment determined in the consequence—is the principle of consequence: this principle then "abysses" [*s'abyme*] or shows some of itself. In short, Condillac explains that, had he followed order itself in composing the *Essay,* he would have discovered more quickly the principle of order. A sentence which, since it can be inverted, encircles history within nature. But look at the considerations on the order of exposition in the *Essay* (I, 2, §107, pp. 102–03; and II, 2, §§45 ff., pp. 333 ff.). Among other things that will be brought into relief is Condillac's silence on the sense of that error which for a long time limited or delayed the generalization of his discovery: "With regard to philosophic works, nothing but order will enable an author to perceive some things that have been forgotten, or others which have not been sufficiently examined. This I have often myself experienced. The present essay, for example, was finished, and yet I did not even then understand the principle of the connexion of ideas in its full extent. This was owing intirely to a passage of about two pages, which was not in its right place" (ibid., II, 2, §47, p. 334). What is the status of this remark, inscribed in the book only when the "present essay, for example, was finished"?

Condillac never retouched the *Essay*.

What two pages were these?[17] Why doesn't Condillac tell us? If these pages here are made to open and not close our reading, must we stop at this point?

[17]Here is the place to remark other missing or previously removed pages—the two signatures of the *Dictionnaire des synonymes*. They disappeared under conditions which make "an accidental disappearance less likely" (Le Roy, Preface, in *OP*, III, p. viii). These signatures might have contained the definition of *sign*, but also such nouns beginning with *s* which hold so many others in their nets [*fils*]: immediately adjacent to *science* and *sign: sense, sensation, sentiment* [*feeling*], *sentir*. Does the *Dictionnaire des synonymes* then open up or fill up its abyss by not defining either *analogy* or *synonym* or *dictionary* or, consequently, that operation, its own, which describes the movement of sense between the primitive sense and the figured sense, the word taken "by extension" or "figuratively"? This last word, like the word *figured*, is defined by the *Dictionnaire* only in its literal or proper sense. The case is rare and significant.

4.

A marginal note or remark—the two loose pages

> "I . . . have given too much to signs."
> "I have said more than I wanted to, than I meant."

Not without having posed — to order our reading, that is, to examine the negativity of the order — the question of the *detour*.

How is a detour possible?

How do we get back from one?

Whether the question there is one of life or death, reason or folly, from now on we are bound to think it.

This can be verified — in my hypothesis — on every page of the *Essay*. Just as an indication, this *reflection* — it was written long after the *Essay* and pertains to its arrival in *Histoire moderne* (in *OP*, II, p. 221):

> Elsewhere I have shown you that the whole art of writing bears on the principle of the greatest connection of ideas, because in fact the art of thinking has no other principle itself. To the extent we are capable of following this connection, our mind is stretched more: it sees each thing in its place; it embraces at once a multitude of objects; and perceiving them clearly, it exposes them with precision.
>
> The more you reflect on the history of the human mind, the more you will be convinced of the universality of this principle. Locke remarked that the false connections of ideas make madness or folly, and he stopped there. Yet it was easy to conclude that the true connection of ideas makes reason. And in reflecting a little on this consequence, this philosopher had seen that this principle is the unique cause of all the mind's qualities.
>
> This path was certainly the shortest one to discover the universality of this principle. And perhaps you believe it is the one I have taken. Not at all. Only just now have I barely

perceived it. And now that I have come to it, I see that I have made great detours.

In short, as we will see, the sign is the name the *Essay* will have given to the detour in general, to experience itself as a detour, the generation of the supplementing [*suppléance*] to be retraced. Now another instance of the abyss, Condillac's recurrent interpretation of the *Essay* does not appear only inside and outside the *Essay* concerning the natural order of ideas.

The interpretation even grapples with the concept of the sign.

Here again, the question is less a critical return bearing on the content of any particular proposition than a general reordering, a rediscovery, and a fundamental reconstitution of the interconnections. In fact, when Condillac wrote the *Essay*, he considered the principal contribution of this book, its most original advance, to be the theory of signs and of the analogy of signs. Now some years later, in 1752 (the *Essay* dates from 1746), Condillac thanks Maupertuis for his *Reflexions philosophiques sur l'origine des langues* and acknowledges he himself was "mistaken."

But it is difficult to determine Condillac's error.

What in effect is "giving too much to signs"? "I would hope that you had shown how the progress of the mind depends on language. I tried that in my *Essay on the Origin of Human Knowledge*, but I was mistaken and have given too much to signs."[18]

---

[18]Letter to Maupertuis, 25 June 1752, in *OP*, II, p. 536. So Condillac had "reflected" on this before Maine de Biran, whose reservation he literally anticipates here: "The more I reflect on the influence that signs and methods have on the art of thinking, the more I am inclined to believe that Condillac has extended

Before concluding from this that "Condillac's thought has evolved" (note of G. Le Roy, in *OP,* II, p. 536), we must prudently analyze this correction. The correction concerns less the order of interconnections than the degree of thematic insistence and the importance accorded to a link nonetheless not out of place. Insistence, force, the quantity or quality of insistence, is not a secondary value in philosophical discourse, and our concern here is not to minimize it. On the contrary, we should no doubt have to theorize and formalize its status. It remains that a variation of insistence, a difference of evaluation is not an alteration of order.

The insistence on the sign was in fact massive. And it does not wait for Part II ("Of language and method"). From Part I ("Of the materials of our knowledge, and particularly of the operations of the soul"), the semiological program of the introduction is largely broached: "And yet I have thought it proper to make this same subject [words] a considerable part of the following work, as well because it may be viewed in a new and more extensive light, as because I am convinced that the use of signs is the principle which unfolds the germ of all our ideas" (*Essay,* Intro., p. 11 [modified]). As soon as the question concerns the connection of ideas (Chapter 3) and of *need,* as the unique principle of our relation to things, Condillac situates those "kind of chains, whose force would intirely consist in the analogy of the signs" (ibid., I, 2, §29, p. 46 [modified]).

---

this influence too far" (Maine de Biran, *Notes sur l'influence des signes,* in *OMB,* I, p. 308). But the "too much of the sign" is not read in the same way in both places. Condillac might not have subscribed to what immediately follows: "he wants to prove (pp. 226–27 of *La Langue des calculs*) that the method of reasoning in metaphysics is not different from the method of calculus in arithmetic or algebra."

·Force, analogy, signification will always be ordered to a theory of need.

Do not hurry too quickly to oppose this to a theory of desire.

And it is still in Part I (long before he expressly discussed language) that the well known distinction is proposed, extremely provisional this time, between the three kinds of signs: accidental signs, natural signs, and instituted signs (ibid., I, 2, §35, p. 51). Much farther on, in the same part of the work:

> This operation is the result of the imagination, which presents signs to the mind with which it had been as yet unacquainted; and of the attention which connects them with our ideas. It is one of the most essential operations in the study of truth; and yet it is one of those which are least known. I have already shewn the use and necessity of signs in acquiring a habit of the operations of the soul. I shall now demonstrate the same thing, considering them in relation to the different species of ideas. This is a truth which cannot be too often exhibited under different views. (Ibid., I, 4, ch. i, p. 114 [modified])

So the *Essay* is through and through a semiotics.

Part II does not open a new field; it unfolds or, if one prefers, folds itself back again over Part I. While treating language, Part II describes only one species of sign, the arbitrary, the one which bears our freedom the highest, the one of which we are the greatest "masters" (this word might be followed as a guiding thread, a clue).

And yet, although semiotics occupies the whole scene or rather the proscenium of all his discourse, Condillac will never have affirmed that the sign is first in experience in general. The chain of signs is raised *over* perceptions ("Over each of these series, other series of ideas might be raised, which should form a kind of chains, whose force would intirely consist in the analogy of the signs, in the order of perceptions, and in the connection that should be formed by the circumstances which sometimes reunite the most dissimilar ideas" [ibid., I, 2, §29, p. 46 (modified)].).

Not only is the chain of signs superstructural, its principle is formal. This chain comes to organize a material and to develop, to distribute a seed. Its operation is always conceived according to this opposition of material and employment. "The use of signs is the principle which unfolds the germ of all our ideas."

Although he devoted a few pages to these, although in sum he gave them too few, Condillac will not have begun any less by describing the elementary materials and operations of the soul. The first three chapters do this. *At the moment* the present object comes to be missing from perception, the moment perception is absent from itself, at that moment the space of signs, with the function of imagination, is opened (ibid., I, 2, §17, p. 38). (But this moment, posed as secondary, as nonprimordial—is it a moment? Is time, which secures this category of the moment, not that very thing which *absents* perception?) In the order of experience and of the operations of the soul, the sign then is never (*posited*) at the beginning. The *Treatise on the Sensations* which will restore the balance of the insistence does not correct the *Essay*, does not reorder things. It "retraces" the generation by going further back to the first knowns, to *practical knowledge*. Practical knowledge does not need signs or language. The *Essay*, as we recall, is a treatise on the understanding (and not the will— another matrical opposition); it concerns *theoretical knowledge* and distinct ideas. These last two need signs or language. Just as the language of action precedes and grounds all language (the thesis of the *Essay* that will never be called into question again), so practical knowledge precedes theoretical knowledge. And in the logical order, which is not time's, the treatise on the sensations precedes the essay on the origin of human knowledge: "We must distinguish, however, as I have already pointed out, theoretical from practical knowledge. Now theoretical knowledge requires a language, because it consists in a sequence of distinct ideas and consequently has need of signs to classify and determine them. Practical knowledge on the other hand consists of confused ideas which rule our actions without letting us remark how they make us act" (*TS*, IV, Intro., p. 195 [modified]).[19]

[19]In this philosophy of consciousness, in this phenomenology of perception, the value of *remark* very often plays in a more or less apparent fashion a discriminating role. Here the capacity to "remark" seems to distinguish theoretical knowledge from practical knowledge. The latter gives rise to some "confused ideas." Does re-marking such ideas afford them clarity and theoretical dignity? Before the *Treatise on the Sensations*, the *Essay* (which opens with a criticism of Leibniz) does not admit the existence of obscure and confused ideas ("For this reason I think, that to have clear and distinct ideas is, in a more concise way of speaking, really to have ideas; and to have obscure and confused ideas, is to have none at all" [I, 1, §13, p. 24].). "There are therefore no perceptions in the soul, of which it does not take notice. Hence perception and consciousness are only the same operation under two different names" (ibid., I, 2, §13, p. 35 [modified]). We ought not to conclude in favor of a contradiction, or even an evolution: the *Essay* analyzes understanding and theoretical knowledge; its object is only *remarked* ideas, hence clear and distinct ones. There are no others at all in the theoretical order.

If we wanted to follow the complex and always open course of the relation to Leibniz, the notion of *remark* could organize one of the possible readings. At least concerning the problem of unconsciousness: if the knowledge Condillac could have of Leibniz was generally very insufficient, it was null in the particular region of their greatest proximity (universal characteristic and language of calculus, and so on). Reconsidering his interpretation of Leibniz apropos obscure ideas, Condillac, in a letter to Cramer, makes all the *critical* force of his argumentation bear on the original possibility of *remarking*: "Taking notice [*prendre connaissance*] belongs to consciousness, and remarking to attention. The example I give of what happens in a man who reads seems convincing to me" (*Lettres*, p. 82). As for what concerns

Signs classify and enlighten. Are they, for all that, without force? There is also a force, a quantity of the analogy of signs. And we must ask ourselves what relation there is between practical force and the theoretical force which comes in short to *remark* how the confused ideas regulating our actions, how prelinguistic and presemiotic judgments and mute analysis "make us act." For there is idea, judgment, analysis before all signification. By signification, we must understand activity, activation itself, activation by putting into an articulatable chain, signification as concatenation, concatenation as distinction. Before signification, sensation analyzes, judges, knows, but in confusion and obscurity, say in the natural light of instinct.

---

the criticism of Leibniz, we must refer above all to the *Traité des systèmes*. The operation of remarking in the "man who reads" (the choice of this example cannot be insignificant) is analyzed from the first pages of the *Essay*, but the word *remark* is still not inscribed in it. The concept is very clearly at work there and determined as consciousness taking notice of a remarkable though nonremarked consciousness, a conscious actualization of a subconscious consciousness.

Remarking is remarked against unconsciousness in general: "If we reflect on ourselves the moment after we have been reading, it will appear to us as if we had had no consciousness but of the ideas which that reading has produced. We shall no more imagine that we had a perception of every letter, than that we have a perception of darkness so often as we involuntarily close our eyelids. But this appearance cannot impose upon us, when we come to reflect that without a consciousness of the perception of letters, we should not have been conscious of the words, nor consequently of the ideas" (*Essay*, I, 2, §9, p. 32). As with all of Condillac's concepts, those of consciousness, unconsciousness, remark, and so on, the gap or deviation is not that of a structural opposition but of a difference of degree: a subtle, gradual, infinitely differential transition from one quality to another, as from one quality then back to itself again. Attention to difference, always at the risk of empiricism—and of occult force. Knowledge is never absent, only more or less slight: "Now if by consciousness of a perception is understood reflected knowledge which fixes the remembrance of it, then obviously most of our perceptions escape our consciousness. But if by that is understood knowledge which, though too slight to leave any traces after itself, is nevertheless capable of influencing and in fact influences our conduct the moment perception becomes experienced, there is no doubt that we are conscious of a multitude of perceptions which seem not to notify us of their presence. Some examples will clarify my

But reason *is* instinct. As there is between reason and instinct only a difference of degree, the two concepts, here again, do not oppose each other. And yet reason *is not* instinct. The difference of degree (analogy, then) produces and destroys the *is* of every predication, supports and deports at once each ontological statement. And already every metaphysical determination or delimitation. For example, the alleged sensationalism and all recourse to a primordial principle. What simultaneously constructs and ruins such a discursive edifice can be analyzed: "The faculty of feeling is the first among all the soul's faculties; it is even the sole origin of the others; and the sentient being does nothing but transform itself. In the beasts there is that degree of intelligence we call *instinct*, and in man that higher degree we call *reason*" (*Traité des animaux*, in *OP*, I, p. 379).

Thus the statue has a method, and nothing in the *Essay* ever excluded this. Whatever progress it makes in reflecting on itself, in the exactitude and clarity of the analysis, in philosophy and in the language of calculus, method never

---

thought" (*De l'art de penser*, in *OP*, I, p. 723). We probably should examine the fact that none of the three announced examples returns to a "natural" perception but to reading once more, to a theatrical scene, and to the painted picture.

Dictionnaire des synonymes: "REMARK. n. See *Note*.

"REMARK. v. *To mark*, as it were, a second time, i.e., to see with a particular attention what escapes or what is supposed able to escape others and is thought useful to recall. See *Observe*."

Thus from remark we are referred to observation, the ultimate recourse and value of this philosophy. And to *note* as semio-gnoseological unity: "NOTE. n. From *noscere notum*, to know. Mark by which a thing is recognized or designated. But this name is particularly given to certain characters proper for abridging writing. There are some for chemistry, astronomy, algebra, and so on, without speaking of musical *notes*, which are sufficiently known. *Note d'infamie* (a mark or brand of infamy) is said figuratively.

"*Note, mark, sign, signal, nota, enseigne. Sign* is the general term and is said of everything proper to indicate a thing. *Mark* is a sign that is natural to the thing, i.e., a sensible quality by which a thing is recognized. *Note* is an arbitrary sign. . . ."

does anything but develop the mute material of sensation, the practical method and tacit analysis of the statue.

> Its method of acquiring them [ideas] is to observe succes-
> sively, one after the other, the qualities it attributes to
> objects. It analyses naturally but it has no language. Now an
> analysis which is carried on without signs can only give very
> limited cognitions. They are necessarily few in number, and
> because it has not been possible to put them into order the
> collection of them must be very confused. When I treat,
> then, of the ideas which the statue acquires I do not claim
> that it has [the French continues: cognitions for which it can
> give an exact account: it has only] practical cognitions. All
> the light it has is really instinct, that is to say, the habit of
> directing itself by ideas for which it does not know how to
> account. This habit, once contracted, guides it surely, with-
> out it having the need to recall the judgments which made it
> contract the habit. In a word it has acquired ideas. But once
> ideas have taught it to guide itself, it thinks no more, it acts
> by habit. To acquire theoretical cognitions it must necessar-
> ily have a language: for it must classify and define ideas,
> which supposes that signs are employed with method. (See
> the first part of my grammar, or my logic.) (*TS*, II, 8, §35, p.
> 116)

To account for, to "give an exact account" of: the fre-
quency of this figure urges us on as much as the whole
system. From the most natural articulation up to the greatest
formality of the language of calculus, the sign's function is to
"account for," is to give the *ratio* to itself according to its
calculative essence. But this calculus remarks, its force repeats a force older than itself, on the side of action, passion,
need. The theoretical is only a supplying remark [*une remar-
que suppléante*] of the practical.

So Condillac simultaneously forewarns against a semio-
linguisticist interpretation of his system (including the *Essay*)
and against a reading of history as the history of discourse,

indeed as an autonomous history of discursive statements. In going back to the presemiotic stratum of practical need, he wants to institute or restore all scientific languages, all theoretical discourses: because they are made of signs and values, above all when they treat signs and values (psychology, linguistics, semiology, rhetoric, history of ideas, history of science, and so on). In each case we can transpose the intent that opens *Le Commerce et le gouvernement considérés relativement l'un à l'autre* (1776): to produce the language of a new science by going back to its principle, here the "foundation of the value of things" in the system of (natural and factual) needs or wants. "Each science demands a particular language, because each science has ideas which are peculiar to it. It seems that we should begin by fashioning this language: but we begin by speaking and writing, and the language remains to be created. That is the state of the science of economics, which is the object of this very work. Among other things, we propose to make up for that, to supply that" (in *OP*, II, p. 242).

As long as the defects of language will not have been supplied, the alleged discourse of a science, for example that of economics in 1776, is condemned to remain an "indecipherable cipher" (note added after the first edition, ibid.).

To supply a language's defects is a *theoretical* and *methodical* operation of *remarking*. Wherever such an operation takes place—that is, everywhere, when the present comes to present itself, to do away with itself in its time—this operation remarks the anteriority in fact, of the *fact* (in the beginning was action, practice: in the beginning, i.e., in nature) as anteriority on itself of what comes to be lacking in itself. The analogy (to itself) ties this anteriority to that lack. To supply is, after having remarked and "retraced" the origin of the lack, to add what *is necessary*, what *is missing* [*il faut*]. But what *is necessary* — what is lacking — also presents itself as a surplus, an overabundance of value, a frivolous futility that would have to be subtracted, although it makes all commerce possible (as sign and value). Several consequences:

1. Learning always amounts, through a remarking supplementation [*par suppléance remarquante*], to recognizing what is already known, *in practice*. Here language is an example *and* the environment of this process. The harm (too much missing) always results from this practical precipitancy of language (first and always of action) which precedes itself, speaks before knowing (itself) how (to speak). "I will have more than one occasion to observe that the difficulty of making good elements comes in part from a language which has been badly made, which we persist in speaking because it was spoken before us" (*La Langue des calculs,* in *OP*, II, p. 423). "Thus in calculating will we learn to calculate, as in speaking we learned to speak. We would live a long time before knowing our language, or we would never even know it, if we wanted to speak only after having each time consulted our grammar. Nature does not instruct us that way: what it wants to teach us it makes us do. . . . I am not supposed to make these signs known to them [the beginners]: they are supposed to see the signs in what they know, and I answer them that they will discover these signs" (ibid., p. 425). A reminder to every future science or theory of language that it will always have to draw on this *fact*, on this observable: there is language and it is spoken as it is spoken. No rule, no transgression of the rule extends beyond the factuality of that fact.

2. Given the overabundance of value and the frivolous futility necessarily produced by the operation of supplemen-

tation or supplying [*suppléance*], the economic and the semio-linguistic sciences are no more juxtaposed than subordinated to each other. Their overlapping and cross-checking within a general theory of need and overabundance, of utility and nonutility, draw a more complex figure. First, a reciprocal figuration wherein each goes round the other. Thus, just now you read a proposition on the necessity to remake the language of economics in order to constitute the science of economics. This proposition opened the treatise on *Le Commerce et le gouvernement* (*commerce* is also regularly used by Condillac in the sense of social and linguistic exchange; see the opposition commerce/trade in the *Dictionnaire des synonymes*). Here now is the final proposition of the *Traité des systèmes*:

> When you study a new science (if it is well laid out), its beginnings ought to be as easy as can be: for it leads you from the known to the unknown. So you are made to find in your knowledge itself the first things you are made to remark, and it seems you knew them before you learned them.
>
> . . . But remark that you have a language to learn, and that a language is not known because its words were once seen: it is necessary to speak it. . . .
>
> Yet a difficulty remains, and it is a great one. It derives from this: before having studied the sciences, you already speak a language, and you speak it badly. For, besides some words which are new to you, their language is your language. Now you agree that you often speak your own language without you yourself understanding what you say, or that, at best, you almost understand yourself. However, that is enough for you and for others, since they pay you with the same money. In order to maintain our conversation, we tacitly seem to agree that in our conversation words take the place of ideas, as in play tokens take the place of money. And, even though a cry is raised against those imprudent enough to play without being informed of the

tokens' value, anyone can with impunity speak without
having learned the value of words.

Do you want to learn the sciences with ease? Begin by
learning your own language. (In *OP*, I, pp. 216–17)

The effect of overabundance produced by what supplies
the lack gives rise to commerce, both economic and linguistic, as well as to trade and to the frivolity of chitchat. This
effect produces in both fields the same objects: merchandise,
money, the token or idea, the full sign, the empty sign.

But founded on need alone, this economy can nevertheless function, or at least trade, only insofar as it produces a
useless supplement, an overabundance [*une surabondance*].

Marx, as is known, first denounces a confusion between
use value and exchange value.

> Hence, we see that behind all attempts to represent the
> circulation of commodities as a source of surplus-value,
> there lurks a *quid pro quo*, a mixing up of use-value and
> exchange-value. For instance, Condillac says: "It is not true
> that on an exchange of commodities we give value for value.
> On the contrary, each of the two contracting parties in every
> case, gives a less for a greater value. . . . If we really ex-
> changed equal values, neither party could make a profit.
> And yet, they both gain, or ought to gain. Why? The value of
> a thing consists solely in its relation to our needs. What is
> more to the one is less to the other, and *vice versâ*. . . . It is not
> to be assumed that we offer for sale articles required for our
> own consumption [: it is our overabundance]. . . . We wish to
> part with a useless thing, in order to get one that we need; we
> want to give less for more. . . . It was natural to think that, in
> an exchange, value was given for value, whenever each of
> the articles exchanged was of equal value with the same
> quantity of gold. . . . But there is another point to be consid-
> ered in our calculation. The question is, whether we both
> exchange something superfluous [*surabondant*] for some-
> thing necessary." We see in this passage, how Condillac not
> only confuses use-value with exchange-value, but in a really

103

childish manner assumes, that in a society, in which the production of commodities is well developed, each producer produces his own means of subsistence, and throws into circulation only the excess over his own requirements. Still, Condillac's argument is frequently used by modern economists, more especially when the point is to show, that the exchange of commodities in its developed form, commerce, is productive of surplus-value.[20]

Condillac kept the case [*instance*] of the sign in its place, in order. And so little did he feel any need to question again the content of his theory "of the necessity of signs" that he recalls in *De l'art de penser* (in a note after 1775): "Since the printing of my *Essay on the Origin of Human Knowledge*, from which the greatest part of this work is drawn, I finished demonstrating the necessity of signs, in my *Grammar* and *Logic*" (in *OP*, I, p. 731).

Will the *Essay*, then, have put into place an unbreakable, only transformable, machine, one henceforward engaged in an uninterrupted movement? There are too many presuppositions in such a question. Let us say that here we would have to examine pieces rather than rush toward any response.

What most *resembles* a rupture from the *Essay* to the *Treatise on the Sensations* is abandoning an "idealist" conception of the structure of sensibility.

Here the word "idealist" is not one of those ample readymade garments which are loosely hung on the philosophers we would never be able to read.

First a citation from Diderot:

---

[20]*Capital: A Critical Analysis of Capitalist Production,* trans. Samuel Moore and Edward Aveling, ed. Frederick Engels, Vol. I, Part II, Ch. 5: "Contradictions in the General Formula of Capital" (Moscow: Foreign Languages Publishing House, 1961), pp. 159–60 [modified].

Those philosophers, madam, are termed *idealists* who, conscious only of their own existence and of a succession of [in]ternal sensations, do not admit anything else; an extravagant system which should to my thinking have been the offspring of blindness itself; and yet, to the disgrace of the human mind and philosophy, it is the most difficult to combat, though the most absurd. It is set forth with equal candour and lucidity by Doctor Berkeley, Bishop of Cloyne, in three dialogues. It were to be wished that the author of the *Essay on the Origin of Human Knowledge* would take this work into examination; he would there find matter for useful, agreeable, and ingenious observation—for which, in a word, no person has a better talent. Idealism deserves an attack from his hand, and this hypothesis is a double incentive to him from its singularity, and much more from the difficulty of refuting it in accordance with his principles, which are the same as those of Berkeley. According to both, and according to reason, the terms essence, matter, substance, agent, etc., of themselves convey very little light to the mind. Moreover, as the author of the *Essay on the Origin of Human Knowledge* judiciously remarks, whether we go up to the heavens, or down to the deeps, we never get beyond ourselves, and it is only our own thoughts that we perceive. And this is the conclusion of Berkeley's first dialogue, and the foundation of his entire system. Would you not be curious to see a trial of strength between two enemies whose weapons are so much alike? If either got the better it would be he who wielded these weapons with the greater address; the author of the *Essay on the Origin of Human Knowledge* has lately given in his *Treatise on Systems* additional proof of his adroitness and skill and shown himself a redoubtable foe to the systematics.

We have wandered far from the blind, you will say. True, madam, but you must be so good as to allow me all these digressions. . . .[21]

---

[21]*Letter on the Blind for the Use of Those Who See*, in *Diderot's Early Philosophical Works*, trans. and ed. Margaret Jourdain (Chicago: Open Court, 1916), pp. 104–05 [modified]. Also see the long passage a little farther on about the question of the born-blind and its interpretation by Condillac (pp. 119 ff.), as well as the notes in Diderot's *Oeuvres Philosophiques*, ed. Paul Vernière (Paris: Garnier, 1964), pp.

In taking into account a criticism, in reinterpreting the operation of the born-blind, in insisting on the priority of touch in the movement of objectification, the *Treatise on the Sensations* contradicts the *Essay* less than its author sometimes seems to think. In fact, the *Mémoire* joined, in the Correspondence, to the *Lettres à Cramer* illuminates Condillac's own reading of the *Essay*. On more than one point and on his relation to Leibniz in particular. Now as to the problem of the born-blind and all it leads to, the author wants to parcel out the "errors": "Locke, Berkeley, and I—all three of us are wrong. As to the reason for this, ask the young lady who made me see this. She will not grant to you or Berkeley that sight all alone can give the idea of surfaces of only two dimensions, and I believe she is right" (*Lettres*, pp. 107–08; also see *TS*, Dedication, pp. xxx and xxxiii).

To insist on the fact that touch is "the only sense which of itself can judge of externality" and which "teaches the other senses to judge external objects" [*TS*, II, p. 73; and III, p. 133], is first to return to the practical base of theoretical knowledge: this was recognized in the *Essay*. Next, it is to try—we do not say succeed—to account for the representative character of the idea: the program for this had been fixed by the *Essay*. The *Essay* did not fulfill this and merely confined itself to the theoretical surface of knowledge. Nevertheless it had clearly posited the representative charac-

---

114–15 and 129 ff. With what eye did Condillac read Diderot's *Letter*? We will judge it with how he wrote to Cramer: "The Prussian oculist [Hilmer, famous for having successfully performed cataract operations] left behind in Paris a rather equivocal reputation; he stayed in Lyon only for the time required to work wonders. I hear he is going to Geneva. I reckon he will be better judged there than elsewhere. If you have any born-blind, I recommend him to you. Are you acquainted with a work by Diderot entitled *Letter on the Blind for the Use of Those Who See*? I will tell you nothing about it for I am praised too much in it" (*Lettres*, p. 54).

ter of sensation as idea, i.e., as relation with the object outside us. "[N]o philosopher ever asserted that they [sensations] were innate; this would have been plainly contradicting experience. But it has been said, that they are not ideas; just as if they were not in themselves as representative as any other thought of the soul" (*Essay*, I, 1, §9, p. 19). "We must therefore distinguish three things in our sensations. 1°. The perception which we feel. 2°. The application we make of it to something without us. 3°. The judgment, that what we apply or attribute to those things, really belongs to them" (ibid., §11, p. 21).

Error and obscurity can only affect judgment. It follows that the representativeness itself is in us, wherein it finds the condition of its clarity and certainty. So grounding this representativeness on touch, as the *Treatise* will do,[22] will not suffice to escape strictly the accusation of idealism. The question affects very little. We could say that the *Treatise* corrected the *Essay*'s idealism. We can say as well that the *Treatise* confirms it. Or that the *Essay* never advanced the least idealist thesis. How is this whole combination of statements

---

[22]For example, when defining the idea itself in its representative structure, Condillac states that the objectivity of the idea (as well as, it must be added, of the language of calculus) controls with the finger rather than the eye; and that sensation becomes idea only by force of touch: "The word *idea* expresses a thing that no one, I must say this, has yet explained well. That is why there are disputes on their origin.

"A sensation is still not at all an idea, to such an extent that it is considered to be only a feeling, which is simply content to modify the soul. . . . Present sensations of hearing, taste, sight, and smell are only feelings, when these senses have not yet been instructed by touch, because the soul then can only grasp them as modifications of itself. . . . The present, like the past, sensation of solidity is by itself alone both feeling and idea. It is feeling by the relation it has to the soul which it modifies; it is idea by the relation it has to something outside.

"This sensation soon forces us to judge as outside ourselves all the modifications the soul receives through touch, and that is why each sensation of touch finds itself representative of objects the hand holds" (*Extrait raisonné du Traité des sensations*, in *OP*, I, pp. 333–34).

always possible? Always justifiable? What is its program? Can a new combination arise from it? And is this question of the new combination prescribed or not by Condillac's text?

What is prescribing a question? Opening it? Horizontally closing it off from its response? Abandoning it on the way?

Can questioning be withdrawn, preserved from teleology?

What is teleology concerning the text?

Teleology then. You have already remarked that this alleged Introduction prohibited itself from saying in short anything about the *Essay*, about what we would want to find there as its own proper and ventral content. An introduction should not intrude [*s'introduire*], it should not enter into the text, above all not saturate the text with reading. To introduce is to seduce. To seduce the text of course and not the reader, to deviate the text from itself, but just enough to surprise it again very close to its content, which can always open out as nothing: as a central void, an alarming superficiality, a rigorous "abyss." Because of that, to busy ourselves round about: lines, grating, borders, ribs, architecture, after-cuts [*après-coupure*]. The *Essay* in the spider web of other texts, of the whole text "signed" by Condillac; in its relation to every effect of signing and signature as possible, in its "own," "proper" spider web; in its relation to every effect of property or propriety as possible. Not a formalist reading (let that be said to forestall the small review of prohibitions), but an analysis of the great machine of oppositions (including that of form and content) wherein a text displaces its program: what the text programs, what programs the text, and what on all sides *breaches* the program, limits it in its very own opening, and defeats in advance its teleology, undecides its circle.

Teleology then, in order to suspend the *Essay* one last time on one of its cut-after-the-fact ribs [*nervures après-coupées*].

Apparently the book is divided into two parts of equal length, or almost so: (1) "Of the materials of our knowledge, and particularly of the operations of the soul." (2) "Of language and method." In his own particular Introduction, Condillac explains this partition; there is no use speaking about that here, it is enough to go and see a little farther on.

First, both parts can be thought to balance each other and correspond to two objects placed side by side.

Doesn't Condillac encourage this?

> In order to execute this double object, I have traced things as high as possible. On the one hand, I have ascended to perception, because it is the first operation we can remark in the soul; and I have shewn how, and in what order it produces every other operation of which we can acquire the act and habit. On the other hand, I have begun with the language of action: here the reader will see how it has produced every art proper to express our thoughts; such as gesture, dancing, speech, declamation, arbitrary marks for words or things [*l'art de la noter*], pantomimes, music, poetry, eloquence, writing, and the different characters of language. This history of language will disclose the circumstances in which the signs were imagined, will shew the true meaning of them, will help to prevent the abuse they may be turned to, and, in my opinion, will remove all doubt concerning the origin of our ideas.
>
> At length after laying open the progression of the operations of the soul, as well as that of language, I have attempted to point out the means by which we may avoid falling into error, and to shew the order we ought to follow, either in endeavouring to make discoveries, or instructing others concerning those we have already made. Such is the general plan of this essay. (*Essay*, Intro., pp. 7–8 [modified])

But—secondly—isn't the balance upset on one side? Isn't the part concerning language the other part of the book,

next to the first part concerning the materials of our knowledge? *Part II is part of a whole defined in Part I, so Part I is
already, by itself alone, the whole.* The whole—that is, the system
of perception and of the three kinds of sign. Part II analyzes
the generation and the functioning of the system of instituted signs, only one of the three kinds.

But—thirdly—this kind is not one among others. From the
outset (a rupture of presence at the origin) the whole process
is magnetized toward the greatest *mastery* possible, that is, the
institution of arbitrary signs which are entirely at our *disposal*
or *control*. Let us follow the progress of repetition which
assures passing from perception to imagination and from
one sign to the other: it is on the march toward freedom, the
spontaneity of auto-affection, so that the only true sign, the
complete sign, that from which teleologically proceeds all
natural or accidental signification, is the instituted sign. The
Essay describes this teleological process; Condillac only states
this after the fact [*après coup*]. This certainly appears to be a
correction, a repentance, but it still concerns a teleological
deferred action [*un après-coup*], which reveals in the end an
order of clarification. Methodically, according to the concept
and the practice of this method which shows "the order we
ought to follow" after "laying open the progression of the
operations of the soul, as well as that of language."

There are only arbitrary signs, and signification is the
process of institution. The sign's active essence, its energy, is
freedom.

Such is the *sense* of the *Essay* as reread by Condillac, who
will talk freely about this some years later in a letter to Gabriel
Cramer:

> You want me to explain the prerogative of arbitrary signs
> over natural ones and why the arbitrary signs set free the

operations of the soul that the natural ones leave necessary. That is the most delicate point of my system on the absolute necessity of signs. The difficulty has all its force and is so much better founded since I did not anticipate it. That is what causes me to be a little tangled on this whole matter. I even notice that I have said more than I wanted to, than I meant.

For a moment grant me that, before the use of arbitrary signs, the operations of the soul are not free. The question is proving how they become such by means of those signs.

Let us consider men when they begin to live together. The circumstances in which they find themselves give them the opportunity to establish among themselves arbitrary signs, and the signs make their commerce freer and more extensive, as the opportunity to multiply them further is seized. (*Lettres*, pp. 83–84)

And after having unhooked the chain which ties commerce (the instituted society), the arbitrariness of the sign, freedom, and mastery of the present object, that is, the possibility of manipulating its absence:

On the contrary, before this commerce they only attended to the present object. For what occasion would they have had to think of a need which no longer would have made itself felt? . . . So you see commerce rescues mankind from that state wherein he only attended to the present object which affected him more. . . . So again this commerce begins to draw the soul out of its current state of dependence on objects able to act on the soul, and causes the soul to enjoy its freedom. In Part I, pp. 205, 206, 207 [see *Essay*, I, 4, §25, pp. 132-34], I said things which amount to that.

Now remark that the principle of what derives from commerce lies in the use of arbitrary signs. For how has this commerce begun, how has it expanded itself, preserved itself, if not by means of arbitrary signs?

But, you will ask me, are natural signs nothing? I answer that, until commerce, natural signs are not at all properly signs. (*Lettres*, pp. 84–85)

So the *proper*, the *property* of the sign is the system of the arbitrary. And Condillac always said this. And when he acknowledges he was mistaken, that is to imply his error was only apparent and through an insufficient clearness and a "tangled" exposition, a too much, again, or a too little. He had *always already* said that the sign as such was *always already* destined for the arbitrary, with its whole system of associated values.

The teleology of the rereading is everywhere:

> I answer that, until commerce, natural signs are not at all properly signs. They are only cries accompanying feelings of pain, of joy, and so on, cries which men then actuate by instinct and the conformation alone of the organs. They must live together to have the opportunity to attach ideas to these cries and to employ them as signs. Thus these cries merge with arbitrary signs. I presuppose that in many places, among others, Part I, p. 203, and Part II, pp. 6 and 7 [see *Essay*,I, 4, §§23–24, pp. 131–32; and II, 1, §§2–3, pp. 172–73]. But I seem to suppose the contrary and thereby place too much difference between natural and arbitrary signs. On that I was wrong.
>
> So my whole system on this matter is reduced to the following: Commerce gives the opportunities (1) to change natural cries into signs, and (2) to invent other signs we call *arbitrary*. And these signs (natural as well as arbitrary) are the first principle in the development and progress of the operations of the soul. I admit that on all this my work is not at all sufficiently clear. I expect I will do better another time. (*Lettres*, pp. 85–86)

Thus the possibility of the arbitrary sign governs, but from its end, the totality of the progress. Consequently, articulated language, a system of arbitrary signs, is no longer one region among others within a general semiotics: it is *exemplary*. Articulated language resembles one example among others, it seems to *constitute* one, only one, of the three kinds of signs. Actually, it organizes by orienting, as the best example, the finalized totality of the semiotic process. "Language is the most sensible example of the connexions spontaneously formed" (*Essay*, I, 2, §77, p. 79): Condillac specifies this in Part I of the *Essay* in order to announce that he will treat it in Part II. The object of Part II then will no longer be a particular object: it envelops in advance and draws to itself everything which precedes; it definitively upsets the symmetry to its own benefit. *Part I will have been part of a whole defined in Part II, so Part II remains, once again, by itself alone, the whole.*

5.

Introduction to *An Essay on the Origin of Human Knowledge* — frivolity itself

"Excess, difference, remainder
then are words which signify
precisely the same thing; but
in using them the mental aspects
are not the same."

For an internal reading of the *Essay*, all this—the theory [*spéculation*] of the exemplar, inclusion of the whole in the part—finally returns in the figure of its finality to the *same*: to the powerful circle of an *identical proposition*. Identity in the circle of sense, at least, for the difference of the whole to the part, or the textual surface of the exposition, does not let itself be reduced to that. First of all because such a difference is an "evidence of reason," perhaps even the example of an identical proposition. *De l'art de raisonner*: "The statement *a whole is greater than one of its parts* is still an identical proposition, for it states that a whole is greater than what is not as great as itself. So identity is the sign by which a proposition is recognized as self-evident; and identity is recognized when a proposition can be translated into terms which return to those very terms, *the same is the same*" (in *OP*, I, p. 621).

How can the circle of semantic identity be produced or reproduced through the disclosed difference of the whole to the part? Through the difference of the sign to the idea, of the signifier to the signified? How is such a circle to be considered? How does the *Essay on the Origin of Human Knowledge* involve its text in its thesis?

The reader can be lured into following all the turns of this circle; and not just of the one Rousseau denounces only to step into it more quickly.[23]

---

[23]Here I am referring to the second *Discourse*, to the objection Rousseau addresses therein to Condillac, and to that whole set of problems now well known.

In place of an introduction — to such a circle — our reading can only add more (too much) of an elliptical and frivolous blow.

But under what conditions is frivolity possible?

The form of this question lets itself be disintegrated simply by the very semblance of its object.

Frivolity consists in being satisfied with tokens. It originates with the sign, or rather with the signifier which, no longer signifying, is no longer a signifier. The empty, void, friable, useless signifier. So Condillac says. In the *Dictionnaire des synonymes*, he refers us from *frivolous* to *useless* ("*FRIVOLOUS*. adj. See *Useless*."). *Useless* then: "adj. *vain, frivolous, futile*. Useless is said of things which serve no purpose, are of no use. If they appear to have some utility but are fundamentally useless, they are called *vain*. If their utility bears only on objects of little consideration or worth, they are *frivolous*. As for *futile*, it adds still more to *frivolous* and is said chiefly of reasoning or arguments which bear on nothing."

The sign is *disposability*: if through the imperception and the absence of the thing (time) the sign assures our ideal mastery, puts (as Condillac says) "at our disposal," the sign — fragile and empty, frail and futile — can also, immediately, lose the idea, get lost far from the idea, this time, and not only from the thing, from sense and not only from the referent. Consequently, the sign remains for nothing, an overabundance exchanged without saying anything, like a token, the excessive relief of a defect: neither merchandise nor money. This frivolity does not accidentally befall the sign. Frivolity is its congenital breach: its *entame, archē*, beginning, commandment, its putting in motion and in order——if at least, deviating from itself, frivolity, the sign's disposability, can ever be or present *itself*. Since its structure of deviation prohibits frivolity from being or having an origin, frivolity defies all archeology, condemns it, we could say, to frivolity.

A philosophy of need—Condillac's—organizes all its discourse with a view to the decision: between the useful and the futile.

A philosophy of the sign—Condillac's—always threatens this decision but also expends and multiples itself in order to reduce the threat, always adds "too many signs" in order to efface the gap or fraction. All the negativity subject to the *Essay*'s criticism (bad metaphysics, bad rhetoric, bad language in general) falls under the category of the frivolous: the arrangement of hollow or unnecessary signs. Unnecessary because they do not proceed by identical propositions; hollow because, under the guise of identical propositions, the tautology there is purely verbal, without content, expended in pure loss, without the least idea, that is, without representing the least object, "without object or end, with nothing to say."

Constantly resorting to the values of the same, of analogy, of analysis, of the identical proposition, Condillac had to guard his discourse from frivolity as if from its infinitely alike double. Resembling it, reassembling it, the analog was that positive which produced its negative, the analog of the analog, the useless and vain semblance of discourse, chitchat, the idle tale. Condillac's method consequently consists in indefinitely recharging signs, in saturating semiotics with semantic representation, by including all rhetoric in a metaphorics, by *connecting the signifier*.

Condillac considers metaphor to be the most general concept and the common name of all tropes. That metaphor marks the origin of languages is now a well known thesis of

119

the *Essay*, and the implications of this are very ramified. I will leave this thesis here in the dark: (1) because it is, from a certain perspective, derived from a fundamental analogism; (2) in order to examine it more systematically and closely elsewhere.

Here is how not to be frivolous, between Leibniz[24] and Kant, where the question of the *a priori* synthesis is approached in terms of signs (interminably). And why synonyms do not necessarily make one signifier too many — for the mental aspect [*la vue de l'esprit*] acts in concert:

> *Excess, difference, remainder* then are words which signify precisely the same thing; but in using them the mental aspects are not the same. . . .

---

[24]Does Condillac write, without knowing it, in the margins of a book he has not read? Is his discourse the *frivolous* repetition or the *identification* of Leibniz's statements which themselves are striving to distinguish between identical propositions and frivolous ones, and thus, next, to save metaphysics from a frivolity which gnaws at it from the inside? Will Condillac have plagiarized from Leibniz without knowing it? On that account and in such a case, *La Langue des calculs* would be presented as a part, a piece, an image, or a sheet detached then placed opposite Leibniz's *New Essays Concerning Human Understanding*, as a fragment of this fictive dialogue which itself sets Leibniz over against Locke, the English father of Condillac. Locke's death took away Leibniz's "inclination to publish (his own) remarks on Locke's works." The *New Essays* contain a chapter (VIII) entitled: "Of Frivolous Propositions," which is not found in the book on "Words" but in the book "Of Knowledge."

"OF FRIVOLOUS PROPOSITIONS

"*Ph*[*ilalethes*]. I believe, indeed, that reasonable persons have not been disinclined to employ *identical* axioms in the way of which we have spoken. §2. It also seems that these purely identical maxims are only *frivolous propositions* or *nugatoriae*, as the schools indeed call them. I should not be content to say that they seem thus, did not your surprising example of *the demonstration of conversion* by the mediation of the identicals make me proceed, bridle in hand, thenceforth, when contempt for anything is the question. But I shall tell you that what you allege in their favor proclaims them wholly frivolous; viz.: (§3) you recognize at first sight that they contain no instruction unless to show a man sometimes the absurdity in which he is involved.

120

Let us recall that we can go only from the known to the unknown. Now, how can we go from one to the other? We can because the unknown is found in the known, and it is only there because it is the same thing. So we can pass from what we know to what we do not know only because what we do not know is the same thing as what we know. You who have learned nothing while reading this chapter, you are clearly convinced that everything I said is the same thing as what you knew. Thus when a child will know something, what he will have learned will be the same thing as what he knew.

Now since everything we do not know is the same thing as what we know, we obviously cannot observe too much what we know, if we want to arrive at what we do not know. . . . That is why I begin where no one has ever begun before, and I remark at great length things everybody judges useless to say. I sense I must appear scrupulous about this, but I beg the public to have for me the same indulgence it has for so many others. . . .

"*Th[eophilus]*. Do you count that as nothing, sir, and do you not recognize that to reduce a proposition to absurdity is to demonstrate its contradictory? I indeed believe that you will instruct no man by telling him that he must not deny and affirm the same thing at the same time, but you instruct him by showing him by the force of the consequence, that he does this without thinking of it. It is difficult, in my opinion, always to pass from these *apagogical demonstrations, i.e.* demonstrations which reduce to absurdity, and to prove everything by *the ostensives*, as they are called; and geometers, who are very curious on this point, have tried it sufficiently. Proclus speaks of it from time to time, when he sees that certain ancient geometers, coming after Euclid, have found a demonstration more direct (as they think) than his. But the silence of this ancient commentator sufficiently shows that they did not always accomplish it.

"*§3. Ph.* You will at least admit, sir, that a million propositions may be formed at little expense, but also of very little use; for is it not frivolous to remark, for example, that the oyster is the oyster, and that it is false to deny it, or to say that the oyster is not the oyster? As to which our author agreeably says that a man who would make this oyster sometimes the subject, sometimes the attribute, or the *predicatum*, would justly be like a monkey who should amuse himself by throwing one oyster from one hand to the other, which proceeding could altogether as well satisfy the hunger of the monkey as these propositions are capable of satisfying the understanding of man.

"*Th.* I find that this author, as full of intelligence as gifted with judgment, has every reason in the world for speaking against those who would so use them. But

Perhaps, then, it will be objected that, in the language of calculus, only identical, hence frivolous, propositions are formed. I agree that, in this language as in all the others, only identical propositions are formed, whenever the propositions are true. For having shown that what we do not know is the same thing as what we know, obviously we can only form identical propositions, when we pass from what we know to what we do not know. However, in order to be identical, a proposition is not frivolous.

Six is six is a proposition at once identical and frivolous. But remark that the identity is at the same time in the terms and in the ideas. Now the identity in ideas is not what makes the proposition frivolous; it is the identity in terms. In fact, *there can never be any need* [my emphasis, J.D.] to form this proposition *six is six*; it would lead us nowhere. And frivolity, as we have had the opportunity to remark, consists in speaking to speak, without object or end, with nothing to say.

---

you certainly see how the identicals must be employed to render them useful; viz.: by showing by force of consequences and definitions that other truths which you wish to establish reduce to them.

"§4. *Ph.* I know it and I see clearly that they may be applied with much stronger reason to propositions which appear frivolous and on many occasions are so, wherein a part of the complex idea is affirmed of the object of this idea, as in the statement: *lead is a metal*. In the mind of a man who is acquainted with the meaning of these terms and who knows that lead signifies a very heavy fusible and malleable body, there is this use alone, that in saying metal, you indicate to him at once many simple ideas instead of enumerating them one by one. §5. The same is true when part of the definition is affirmed of the thing defined; as in the statement: *all gold is fusible*, supposing you have defined gold as a yellow, heavy, fusible, and malleable body. Again, to say that the triangle has three sides, that man is an animal, that a palfrey (*palefroy*, an old French word) is an animal which neighs, serves to define the words, but not to teach anything besides the definition. But we learn something from the statement that man has a notion of God and that opium plunges him into sleep.

"*Th.* Besides what I have said of the identicals which are wholly so, we shall find that these semi-identicals have also a particular use. For example, *a wise man is always a man*; that gives us the knowledge that he is not infallible, that he is mortal, etc. Some one in danger needs a pistol-ball, and lacks the lead to found it in the form he has; a friend says to him: remember that the *silver* you have in your purse is *fusible*; this friend will not teach him a quality of the silver, but will make him think of a use he may make of it, in order to have pistol-balls in this pressing need.

It is not the same with this other proposition, *three and three make six*. It is the sum of an addition. So there can be the need to form it, and the proposition is not frivolous, because the identity is solely in the ideas.

It has been supposed, for want of having distinguished two identities, one in words, the other in ideas, that every identical proposition is frivolous, because every identical proposition in words is frivolous in effect. It was never suspected that a proposition would not know how to be frivolous when the identity is only in ideas. No one has even wanted to perceive this identity. For why say, for example, *two and two make four* (why *make*?), if not because *two and two* are thought to be something other than *two and two*: it seems to me one would say *two and two* are *four*, if one had really felt that *two and two* are the same thing as *four*. . . .

When I say they do not remark this identity, I do not mean that they do not perceive it. Who could not perceive it? But if they remarked it, they would be forced to conclude that, when they calculate, they form and can form only identical propositions. Now they object, as if by instinct, to this conclusion, because they have the prejudice that every identical proposition is a frivolous proposition; and they are loath to be frivolous. (*La Langue des calculs*, in *OP*, II, pp. 431–32)

A large part of *moral truths* and of the most beautiful *sentences* of authors is of this nature: they very often teach us nothing, but they make us think at the right time of what we know. That iambic senarius of the Latin tragedy,—

Cuivis potest accidere, quod cuiquam potest,

which might be expressed thus, although less prettily: that which may happen to one, may happen to everybody, only makes us remember the human condition, *quod nihil humani a nobis alienum putare debemus*. This rule of the jurisconsults: *qui jure suo utitur, nemini facit injuriam* (he who uses his own right, injures no one) appears frivolous. But it is very useful on certain occasions and makes one justly think of what is necessary. If, for instance, any one raised his house as far as he is allowed by the statutes and usages, and by so doing deprived his neighbor of some view, he would pay this neighbor at once, according to this rule of law, if he ventured to complain. For the rest, propositions of fact, or experiences, like that which states that opium is a narcotic, carry us farther than the truths of pure

All the more reason, we recall, to teach good metaphysics to calculators. So that they overcome their loathing, most certainly, their prejudice which is like an instinct (reason still bound in instinct), without for all that their becoming frivolous. So that they do not cease to say the same, to remark it at least, but while avoiding "speaking to speak, without object or end, with nothing to say."

Yet just as bad metaphysics begins with language, with the deviation or gap of the futile signifier, with the drift in course by which the sign repeats itself and identifies with itself to signify nothing other than itself, so frivolity arises from the origin of the sign.

That is why philosophical frivolity is not just an accident. Condillac undoubtedly wants to be right about this, which amounts to considering frivolity as a supervening historical evil, which affects from the outside an essentially serious discourse. But simultaneously, according to a logic we have now identified, the accident is also described as a kind of essential fate, structural destiny, original sin.

---

reason, which can never make us go beyond that which is in our distinct ideas. As for this proposition, that every man has a notion of God, it is from the reason, since notion signifies idea. For the idea of God, according to my view, is innate in all men: but if this notion signifies an idea in which you actually think it, it is a proposition of fact which depends on the history of the human race. §7. Finally, to say that a triangle has three sides is not so identical as it seems, for a little attention is required to see that a polygon must have as many angles as sides; it would also have an additional side, if the polygon were not supposed to be closed.

"§9. *Ph.* It seems that the general propositions concerning substances are for the most part frivolous, if they are certain. He who knows the meanings of the words: substance, man, animal, form; vegetative, sensitive, rational soul, will form from them many indubitable but useless propositions, particularly about the soul, of which we often speak without knowing what it really is. Every one may see an infinite number of propositions, reasonings, and conclusions of this nature in the books of metaphysics, scholastic theology, and a certain kind of physics, the reading of which will teach him nothing more of God, spirits, and bodies than he knew before having run through these books.

FRIVOLITY ITSELF

The method for reducing the frivolous is method itself. In order not to be the least frivolous, being methodic suffices.

Order, clarity, precision: not only does logic lack these, but writing too—the philosophical style. Philosophical style congenitally leads to frivolity. But the reason for this is logical, epistemological, ontological. If philosophical writing is frivolous, that is because the philosopher cannot fulfill his statements. He knows nothing, he has nothing to say, and he complicates, subtilizes, refines the stylistic effects to mask his ignorance. Thus he misleads, pays change [*donne change*] out of the essential emptiness of his discourse. When philosophical writing is difficult, esoteric, reserved to a small number, that is because such writing is hollow.

"*Th.* It is true, that abstracts of metaphysics and such other books of this character as are commonly seen, teach only words. To say, for example, that metaphysics is the *science* of being in general, which explains the principles and affections emanating from it; that the principles of being are essence and existence; that the affections are either primitive, viz.: unity, truth, the good, or derivative, viz.: sameness, diversity, simplicity, complexity, etc., and, in speaking of each of these terms, to give only vague notions and verbal distinctions is indeed to abuse the name of *science*. But we must render this justice to the more profound Scholastics, like Suarez (whom Grotius valued so highly) and admit that there is sometimes in them discussions of value, as upon the continuum, the infinite, the contingent, the reality of abstracts, the principles of individuation, the *origo et vacuum formarum,* the soul and its faculties, the concurrence of God with his creatures, etc., and even in ethics, upon the nature of the will and the principles of justice; in a word, we must admit that there is still some gold in these scoriae, but it is only enlightened persons who can profit from it; and to load the youth with the rubbish of inutilities, because there is something of value here and there, would be badly to dispose of the most precious of all things, time. For the rest, we are not wholly destitute of general propositions regarding substances which are certain, and deserve to be known; there are grand and beautiful truths concerning God and the soul which our clever author has taught either in his own right or in part after others. We have perhaps added something also thereto. And as for general knowledge concerning bodies, considerable additions are being made to what Aristotle left, and it should be said that physics, even general physics, has become much more real than it was heretofore. As for real metaphysics, we are beginning, as it were, to establish it, and we find important truths grounded in reason and confirmed by experience, which belong to substances in general. I hope, also, that

125

Poets and orators at an early stage felt the usefulness of method. Thus with them method made the most rapid progress. They had the advantage of trying their productions on a whole people: witnessing the impressions they caused, they observed what was lacking in their works.

Philosophers have not had the same assistance. Regarding writing for the crowd as below them, they have long made it their business to be unintelligible. Frequently this was only a detour for their self-esteem: they wanted to hide their ignorance from themselves, and it was enough for them to seem educated in the eyes of the people who, made more for admiring than for judging, willingly took them at their word. Since, therefore, they have as judges only disciples who blindly adopted their opinions, the philosophers did not have to suspect their method was defective: on the contrary, they had to believe that whoever did not understand them lacked intelligence. That is why their works have produced so many frivolous disputes and contributed so little to the progress of the art of reasoning. (*De l'art d'écrire*, in *OP*, I, p. 592)

The root of evil is writing. The frivolous style is the style—that is written. Unlike the poet and the orator, philosophers (inventors of prose, let us not forget) did not

---

I have advanced a little the general knowledge of the soul and of spirits. Such a metaphysic was the demand of Aristotle, it is the science which he called Ζητουμένη, the desired (*la desirée*) or that which he sought, which must be as regards the other theoretic sciences what the science of happiness is to the arts which it needs, and what the architect is to the workmen. This is why Aristotle said that the other sciences depend upon metaphysics as the most general science and must derive from it their principles, demonstrated by it. You must know also that true ethics is to metaphysics what practice is to theory, because upon the doctrine of substances in common depends the knowledge of spirits and particularly of God and the soul which gives a proper meaning to justice and virtue. For as I have elsewhere remarked, if there were neither providence nor a future life, the wise man would be more limited in the practice of virtue, for he would refer everything merely to his present satisfaction, and even this satisfaction, which appears already in Socrates, in the emperor Marcus Aurelius, in Epictetus and other ancients, would not be so well grounded always without these beautiful and grand views which the order and harmony of the universe open for us even in a future without

"witness . . . the impressions they caused," nor did they find the rule of their discourse in live interchange. Absence of the object, absence of the interlocutor, philosophy, writing, frivolity: where can this chain flag or give way?

Frivolity begins its work, or rather threatens the work of its work in repetition in general, i.e., in the fissure which, separating two repetitions, rends repetition in two. The repetition of the idea, the identity of ideas is not frivolous. Identity in words is frivolous. Condillac undoubtedly says this apropos judgments, sentences, and predicative statements. But he clearly must presuppose this concerning the self-identity of the idea in itself, of the word in itself. The difference between these two identities, thus between these two forces of repetition, would justify the gap or deviation in all its forms between the more and the less, the positive and the negative, notably between the serious and the frivolous. But Condillac has tied the two forces of repetition to one another. Against Locke, he wanted to mark that there was no connection of ideas without the connection of signs. The limit between the two repetitions within repetition itself

---

limits; otherwise the tranquillity of the soul would be only what is called a forced patience, so that we may say that *natural theology*, comprising two parts, theoretical and practical, contains altogether real metaphysics and the most perfect ethics.

"§12. *Ph*. There is doubtless knowledge which is far removed from being frivolous or purely verbal. But this last seems to be that in which two abstracts are affirmed the one of the other; for example, that *parsimony is frugality*, that *gratitude is justice*; and however specious these and other propositions sometimes appear at first sight, yet when we press their force, we find that it all amounts to nothing else than the signification of the terms.

"*Th*. But the significations of terms, *i.e.* definitions united with identical axioms, express the principles of all demonstrations: and as these definitions can make known at the same time the ideas and their possibility, it is plain that what depends on them is not always purely verbal. As for the example that *gratitude is justice*, or rather a part of justice, it is not to be despised, for it shows that what is called *actio ingrati*, or the complaint which can be made against the ungrateful, should be less

cannot be reproduced, stated, or come to signification without engendering that very thing the limit excludes.

Frivolity originates from the deviation or gap of the signifier, but also from its folding back on itself in its closed and nonrepresentative identity. So we escape frivolity only at the semantic risk of nonidentity: Condillac names nonidentity metaphor and makes it the primordial structure of language only in order to begin its analogical and teleological reappropriation. This reappropriation is pursued since the time of the language of action, which opens metaphor, through all the supplying modifications, to the most formal, thus also the most natural, language of calculus. This can be verified, for example, at the beginning of Part II. There we will recognize the hidden guiding thread, the rhetoric of the temporal modes in a narrative which also tells the origin of time and the origin of rhetoric. But well before Part II, time — or the gap of the present relation to itself and still the present's self-relation in iterability — will have named *at once* the root of sensibility and the instance of the frivolous.

Need seems to be the system's unique principle. How does the proposition of need become complicated?

---

neglected in the tribunals. The Romans received this action against the Liberti, or freedmen, and still to-day it should take place as regards the revocation of gifts. For the rest, I have already said elsewhere that abstract ideas also may be attributed to one another, the genus to the species, as in the statements: *duration is a continuity, virtue is a habit*; but *universal justice* is not only *a virtue*, but it is indeed *the complete ethical virtue*" (trans. Alfred Gideon Langley, 2nd ed. [Chicago: Open Court, 1916], pp. 490–97 [modified]).

This repetitive structure of knowing not only gives rise, as we are going to see, to an archeological interpretation of the frivolous but also to a metaphysics of plagiarism—Condillac had suffered much from this accusation (*OP*, I, pp. 222, 318, etc.)—or rather to a theory of metaphysical plagiarism. Note: "Experience has corroborated me in those reflections which I would not have added here, if I had not placed them in the *Essay on the Origin of Human Knowledge*, which I copy in this place as in many others. I still believe I ought to warn that many writers have

In the *Cours d'études* ("Précis des leçons préliminaires"), the definition of desire is placed between that of the understanding and the will. The implication and the reciprocal modification of all these instances frequently remain misleading and confusing. This logic requires, each time, meticulous reconstitutions, if we want to link the different texts among themselves. Here, for example, desire is going to engender or be transformed into will ("faculty which embraces all the operations which arise from need, just as understanding is the faculty which embraces all the operations which arise from attention"). But just as it is at the origin of all knowledge (theoretical and practical) and of attention in general, desire also produces understanding and the theoretical relation with the object.

DESIRE

To be deprived of a thing you judge necessary for yourself produces un-easiness or disquietude in you, so that you more or less suffer: that is called *need*.

The un-easiness determines your sight, touch, all your senses concerning the object you were deprived of. In addition, the un-easiness moves [*détermine*] your soul to

---

copied this Essay, for it could be thought that I myself copied them by writing on the art of thinking. Plagiarizing metaphysicians could not be more common. When they are shown, within themselves, metaphysical truths, they flatter themselves that all by themselves they would have found these truths, and they unscrupulously present these truths to themselves as discoveries. One day Du Marsais complained to me about a shameless plagiarism made from him. I spoke of this to the plagiarist, who replied that *Du Marsais was wrong to complain and that those things there belonged to every good mind or spirit who wanted to attend to them*. Nevertheless those things there escaped the gentlemen of Port-Royal, who were even better minds. For his part an excellent metaphysician, Du Marsais has been one who has created many plagiarizing metaphysicians. Those plagiarists referred to earlier are recognized by the bad metaphysics they form when they are clumsy enough to look without any guide for the facts within themselves" (*De l'art de penser*, in *OP*, I, p. 735n).

attend to all the ideas it has of this object, as well as to the pleasure it could receive from them. So un-easiness determines the action of all the body's and soul's faculties.

This determination of the faculties concerning the object of which one is deprived is called *desire*. Thus desire directs only the soul's faculties if the object is absent; if the object is present, it also includes directing the body's faculties. (In *OP*, I, p. 414; also see *TS*, I, 3, §§1–3, pp. 25–26)

Thus it remains that, although desire in all its force is nothing but need; although the notion of desire is derived from that of need; and although this derivation neither adds nor subtracts any force and only modalizes a need by imparting a direction to it, knowledge (or consciousness) of need passes through desire, through this directed derivation, through the object of this direction. This in particular follows: frivolity—the seeming repetition of desire without any object or of a floating desire—is also need left to itself, need without object, without desire's direction [*rection*]. And so on.

Condillac's *Logic*, which "resembles none of those which have been composed hitherto" (p. 2), does not oppose the logic of need to the logic of desire. On the contrary, the *Logic* is arranged to articulate one to the other or to think them together, as the force and the direction of a moving body [*mobile*]. In Part II of the *Logic* ("Analysis considered in its means and effects, or the art of reasoning reduced to a correct language"), the first chapter is entitled "How The Knowledge We Owe to Nature Forms A System In Which All Is Perfectly United; And How We Stray When We Forget Its Lessons." It opens with the desiring direction of need: "We have seen that by the word *desire* we cannot mean any thing else but the direction of our faculties towards the things which we need. We have therefore only desires, because we

have needs to satisfy. Thus needs and desires are the movers
[*le mobile*] of all our researches" (p. 46 [modified]).

If need is the system's unique principle, if desire is only the
representative vector-ing [*vection*[25]] of need, its relation with
the object the lack of which constitutes it as need, then need
arises and changes into a desiring representation only in the
temporal dehiscence of the comparison.

There is no difference in general, only of degrees. This
fundamental proposition propagates its effects over all of
Condillac's discourse and regularly comes to unfold [*déplier*],
as it were, all the concepts of rupture and repetition. This
unfolding is time's. It is the very origin of need and of the
desiring representation which relates need to an object in
general. Indifference itself is only an effect of (temporal)
comparison, hence an effect of difference.

> §24 *A state is only indifferent by comparison.* Among these
> different degrees there is no state of indifference. At the
> first sensation, howevery [*sic*] feeble it may be, the statue is
> necessarily either contented or discontented. When it has
> felt in succession the sharpest pains and the keenest plea-
> sures, it will judge indifferent, or will cease to regard as
> agreeable or disagreeable, those feebler sensations which
> will appear feebler when compared with the strongest. . . .
> §25 *Origin of need.* Whenever it is ill at ease or less comfort-
> able than it was, it recalls its past sensations and compares
> them with its present, and it feels the importance of becom-
> ing again what it was. From this arises the need, or the
> knowledge it has of a well-being which it judges necessary
> for its comfort.
> It knows of needs only because it compares the pain which

[25][Derrida says of *vection*: " 'Vection' is a rather rare word, if it even exists. Its
sense: the oriented movement of a vector, of what puts in motion and carries in a
direction." Derrida's use of *vection* seems to play off his earlier use (p. 130) of the Old
French word *rection*: direction, governance.—Trans.]

131

it suffers with the pleasure which it has enjoyed. (*TS*, I, 2, pp. 13–14)

As we have noted, the degree, the gradual difference ruins the identical proposition by dislocating the *is*. But at the same time the degree makes the identical proposition possible by giving it a synthetic value which advances knowledge and prohibits frivolity. So time, an element of degree, marks at once the possibility and the impossibility of frivolity. The fragility, the frail structure of the frivolous *is nothing but* (the time of a) difference (of degree), the spacing that ontology, as such, simply could not be capable of. There is a crack there. Construction *and* deconstruction are breached/broached there. The line of disintegration, which is not straight or continuous or regular — philosophy is affected by this almost by itself. Philosophy deviates from itself and gives rise to the blows that will strike it nonetheless from the outside. On this condition alone, at once internal and external, is deconstruction *possible*.

Without the comparison, without time which destroys the table, there would be neither the opposition pleasure/pain (the principle of the principle[26]), nor analogy in general. Without time there would be no object. The gap or deviation of time (repetition and absence of the perceptual present to itself) opens the representative vector-ing within both the sign and the idea. The operation of supplying [*suppléance*] — the concept and the word reappear regularly — is interpreted as representation. Now the sign's vacancy — a frivolous

---

[26]See *TS*, I, 1 and 2, pp. 3 ff. There again the relation to time (to the absence of the present) is posited as the origin of desire. In the fiction of a pretemporal affect, desire remains of stone. "As yet it [the statue] has no idea of change, succession, duration. It exists, then, without being able to form desires" (ibid., 2, §3, p. 5).

one—the suspension of its relation with the object, inter-venes before the sign. Or rather, the sign announces itself before the sign: already on the threshold of generalization or abstraction, that is, as early as this process of extending sense which permits taking a sign "figuratively," inscribes metaphor in the poetic origin of language, and rules the dictionary of synonyms. A "stretched" sense always risks being empty, floating, slackened in its relation with the object. That is why, just as there are two metaphysics, two barbarisms, two imaginations, two identities, we never es-cape the double or stand-in for the idea itself. This is frivoli-ty's last or first garment: "We fall into error on this subject when we suppose that the word *idea* has only one meaning. However, it has two; one which is proper to it and another given it by extension. If I say one pebble, two pebbles, the word idea is taken properly or literally, for I find the ideas of *one* and *two* in the objects I have joined to these names. But if I say *one, two*, they are just general names, and only by extension can they be called ideas" (*La Langue des calculs*, in *OP*, II, p. 430). What is said by extension is always said improperly: "improperly or by extension," Condillac often says (ibid., p. 433).

The frivolous extension which leaves the idea without the thing and the sign without the idea, which lets the term's identity fall far from its object—the identity of the idea, this extension increases with progress itself. It follows the tele-ological movement and extends to the limit of what it disin-tegrates. To the limit, for example, of commerce, of lan-guage, and of institution. Now in the order of the arbitrary, the frivolous instance results from a supplementary compli-cation of the "moving body" (need/desire) which we have not yet taken into account.

On the one hand, frivolity could be thought to come from need through desire: desire opens the direction of the object, produces the supplying [*suppléante*] sign which can always work to no effect [*à vide*: on empty, in a vacuum], by means of vacancy, disposability, extension. More especially since, by itself alone, as an orientation without intrinsic force, desire is essentially slight, thin and inconsistent, inconstant.

On the other hand, and conversely, need in itself is frivolous. Need without desire is blind. It has no object, is identical to itself, enclosed in itself, tautological and autistic. Of stone. By relating need to an object, desire would mobilize it, moralize it, subject it to the law, fix it in an order.

But to remain content with such an opposition of desire and need, however chiasmatic it may be, is to forget that with the human order (the second first — metaphysics as humanism), with language, the arbitrary sign, commerce in general, the chiasmus bends with a supplementary deflection: *the need to desire*.

This need, which is not a desire, does not belong to nature. Or if it does belong to nature — to man's — it is as the ability to acquire. The *Traité des animaux* explains from what "difference alone arise for us the pleasures and pains of which the animals could not form ideas":

> [I]t is no longer possible to fulfill all our desires. On the contrary, since they give us the enjoyment of all the objects to which they carry us, we would be powerless [*on nous mettrait dans l'impuissance*] to satisfy the most pressing of our needs, that of desiring. This activity would be removed from our soul, an activity which has become necessary to the soul. There would remain for us only an overwhelming void, an ennui of everything and of ourselves.
>
> So desiring is the most pressing of all our needs: thus no sooner is one desire satisfied than we form another. Fre-

quently we obey several at once, or, if we cannot do that, we save for another time those to which present circumstances do not permit us to open our soul. Thus our passions renew, succeed, multiply themselves, and we live only to desire and only inasmuch as we desire. (In *OP*, I, p. 372).

No longer is desire the relation with the object, but the object of need. No longer is desire a direction, but an end. An end without end bending need into a kind of flight. This escape sweeps away the origin, system, destiny, and time of *need* (an exempt [*franc*] word and a concept without identity).

The moment the statue awakens, it likewise sets to work to reduce the gap. Stone [*Pierre*] beginning to produce—in order (not) to become again what it will have been, contrary to the frivolous distraction—the headstrong identities of signs, other frivolities: the fear of a Medusa, legitimacy itself.

Index

137